Mysteries, Legends and Myths

of the First World War

Canadian soldiers in the trenches and in the air

CYNTHIA J. FARYON

Formac Publishing Company Limited
Halifax

Formac Publishing Company Limited recognizes the support of the Province of Nova Scotia through the Department of Communities, Culture and Heritage - Creative Industries Fund. We are pleased to work in partnership with the Province of Nova Scotia to develop and promote our cultural resources for all Nova Scotians. We acknowledge the support of the Canada Council for the Arts, which last year invested $153 million to bring the arts to Canadians throughout the country. This project has been made possible in part by the Government of Canada.

Cover design: Shabnam Safari

Library and Archives Canada Cataloguing in Publication

Faryon, Cynthia J., 1956-, author
    Mysteries, legends and myths of the First World War :
Canadian soldiers in the trenches and in the air / Cynthia J. Faryon.

Previously published: Toronto: J. Lorimer, 2009.
Includes bibliographical references and index.
Issued in print and electronic formats.
ISBN 978-1-4595-0488-2 (softcover).--ISBN 978-1-4595-0489-9 (EPUB)

    1. World War, 1914-1918--Canada. 2. World War,
1914-1918--Personal narratives, Canadian. 3. Soldiers--Canada--
Biography. 4. Airmen--Canada--Biography. I. Title.

D547.C2F37 2017   940.4'0971   C2017-903284-4
                                             C2017-903285-2

Formac Publishing Company Limited
5502 Atlantic Street
Halifax, Nova Scotia, Canada
B3H 1G4
www.formac.ca

Printed and bound in Korea.

CONTENTS

This book I dedicate to my newest grandchildren — Aiden, Tristan and Isaac. My ultimate hope is that none of you will ever have to experience war. And a special dedication of Chapter 9 — to my daughter Robin.

PROLOGUE

I've got a feeling in the pit of my stomach that I'm not going to survive the day. I hope it's only the usual fear and the strain of the inhuman conditions getting to me: the mud, exploding shells, human body parts flying through the air — and always, always being wet.

Some days I almost wish for a bullet before I rot away from the mould. It's growing on my feet, in my crotch and even under my arms. But then I think of my home in Manitoba and my angel of a wife.

Earlier today, after the regular morning "stand-to," I wrote her a letter. If I don't survive, I hope someone will make sure she gets it. I folded the letter and tucked it into my helmet.

Oh my God, the shelling has started and look — smoke is covering no-man's-land, and I can see the enemy cutting through the rolls of barbed wire between us and them!

There are more Germans coming at us than I can count. They look like apparitions in this mist — apparitions with bayonets. I'm shooting, and all down the line machine guns are chattering and men are falling. The water in the bottom of the trench is turning red with blood. There are bodies everywhere and wounded men are moaning.

There's a lull and the first rush is over. I'm reloading my gun. Someone's yelling. I look up from the trench and see the dark shadows of the second wave running towards us. I finish loading and take up my position at the parapet. My heartbeat almost drowns out the thudding of ammunition peppering the dirt around me.

I sense the bullet before feeling it.

In stunned disbelief I look at my chest, at the hole and the blood. I look around for help, but my buddies are busy fighting for their own survival. I'm light-headed and don't know what to do. I hold my helmet to my chest to stem the flow of blood, the helmet that holds my last words to my sweet wife. My knees feel weak and I can feel myself falling. I'm helpless to stop what is happening.

Darkness. I feel my body hitting the ground.

What next? Death is coming quickly and I'm engulfed in painless warmth. Then, with a flickering consciousness, I'm leaving my body. The fear is gone and I'm strangely emotionless.

Far off, as if I'm listening through a long tunnel, I hear the scream of flying shells. The sun is shining and I'm drawn to the light. I'm running towards it, elated.

My shadow ripples along the ground beside me. A voice tells me to jump. I'm flying up through clouds. I'm riding the currents. I'm dipping and floating as if I'm in an ocean. I soar as one wave of wind flings me to the next. All around me, the infinity is filled with radiance. Wherever I look light explodes in bursts of colour. I want to stay here forever.

But I can't leave my wife!

The memory of Rita dissolves the blissful images and I'm suddenly back on the dark, blood-soaked ground of this place called Ypres. I stand beside my broken body, which lies in the mud with countless other corpses. I try to identify with the lump of mangled flesh at my feet and will myself to breathe.

I, Edgar Simpson, must go home — home to my wife.

INTRODUCTION

There had been rumours of war long before June 28, 1914, when Archduke Franz Ferdinand, heir to the throne of the Austro-Hungarian Empire, was assassinated in Sarajevo, Bosnia. The assassination simply set the wheels in motion. The war the Allies thought would be over by Christmas plagued the world from August 1, 1914 to November 11, 1918. While it raged it was called the Great War. When it was over it was called the War to End All Wars. When the next European war began 20 years later it became known as the First World War or World War I.

This book tells some of the many Canadian stories that came out of the Great War, and features some legendary battles. Some of these accounts may have been generated in the shell-shocked minds of men who had lost touch with reality, and others from heartbroken civilians who had lost loved ones. But many probably originated because communication both on and off the battlefield was so poor. By the time "facts" reached home, many of them had become distorted or embellished. Another source of these legends was the rumours that both sides started deliberately. They were pure propaganda and victimized not only the enemy they were intended for, but also the news-starved civilians at home.

The war touched many corners of the world, but the stories in this collection concern the action in Europe. Most of them are about trench warfare on the Western Front and all of these accounts feature Canadians — the famous as well as the unsung heroes.

Chapter 1

SAVED BY THE WORD OF GOD

For the first time in history, the whole world was at war. The news rippled through the small community of Albion on Prince Edward Island like a wave. Posters started appearing in shop windows and at the post office. Charlottetown opened a recruitment centre and soon young men in uniforms could be seen everywhere.

News of the war was on everyone's lips and on everyone's mind. The Germans had to be stopped, and Britain needed Canadians to help them win the war. Canada was only too eager to comply, and all over the nation men signed up.

When Chrystie Jenkins thought about the war, which was most of the time, it caused shivers of excitement to course through his body. It consumed his daytime hours and filled his nighttime dreams. He could hardly wait to get his hands on the weekly newspaper and read about battles with foreign names

RMS Olympic. *Her "dazzle" paint job makes her outlines confusing.*

in countries he could only imagine. But he wasn't satisfied simply reading and hearing about the war. He wanted to be there. He wanted to wear a uniform and have the girls hang on his every word. He wanted people to think he was a man. He wasn't a child. He was 16 and he didn't intend to be left behind with the women, children, and old people.

His older brothers had been among the first to go down to the recruitment centre in Charlottetown and sign up. They had gone for training and were already overseas. His parents were worried sick, and his mother combed the papers for news.

Chrystie wasn't worried about his brothers' safety. He was jealous.

Before too long, lists appeared in the local papers naming those missing or killed in action, and memorial services were held in the small local churches. There were no burials because there were no bodies. Families had to mourn their children knowing they were buried in foreign soil — if they were lucky — or simply missing and presumed dead. But that

How WWI pictures were made. Official Canadian War Records Office cameraman William Rider-Rider in the trenches near Lens, France.

wasn't the worst of it. Soon soldiers with missing limbs began coming home.

None of this deterred Chrystie. His yearning grew stronger with every passing day.

His brothers wrote long letters home. Chrystie read their descriptions of the trenches in France, and he knew about the horror of watching friends being shot and seeing human body parts flying all over the place. The newspaper reports told how the wounded would lie in the dirt for hours before being evacuated to aid stations. The casualties were already in the thousands, but still he wanted to go.

13th Battalion Scots in a trench, cleaning a Lewis gun.

There was glory and honour in serving your country, thought Chrystie, and the girls loved a man in uniform. Soldiers were heroes, and that's what he wanted to be — a hero.

Like hundreds of other young Canadian boys, Chrystie sneaked down to the recruitment station and lied about his age. He was accepted and assigned to the Canadian Expeditionary Force with the 5th Siege Artillery Draft as a gunner.

With his blue eyes sparkling he went home to tell his family that he was more than Chrystie Jenkins, the son of Robert Jenkins from Prince Edward Island. He was officially Private Chrystie Jenkins of the Canadian Army, service no. 2040194 and due to ship out overseas on the S.S. *Olympic*. He was a man!

An army has to be fed. Two horse-drawn carts and a truck bring yet more boxes of supplies to add to the mountain at a rear-area depot.

His family was in shock. Chrystie all but danced with pride and excitement. He laughingly told them how he had lied about his age and that no one had questioned him on it.

The day he was to ship out, however, Chrystie received an embarrassing surprise. Someone had told the recruitment centre exactly how old he really was, and Chrystie was told he had to wait until his 17th birthday before they would let him leave.

Chrystie was furious. His family was elated. They hoped the war would be over by the time he was old enough to ship out, and Chrystie would be saved the horrible experience of war. As long as their prayers kept their other boys safe, the family would never have to experience the ordeal of a bodiless memorial service.

His parents' hope was short-lived. The war continued and Chrystie finally turned 17. To his delight, he was permitted to

One of the Royal Highlanders of Canada cleans his new Lee Enfield, a welcome replacement for the finicky Canadian Ross rifle.

ship out right before Christmas 1916. Once in Europe, he was transferred to the 12th Siege Battalion, which was to reinforce the 3rd Battalion of the Canadian Garrison Artillery. He was revelling in the experience. Everything was new and exciting. Chrystie was even fascinated by the kit the army issued him in England. It contained sewing materials, field dressings and a small New Testament bible.

Chrystie put the bible in his front breast pocket.

In May 1917, he joined his brothers in France and learned first hand what life in the trenches was really like. It didn't take Chrystie long to realize that all the grim stories were true. The trenches were nothing but mud — black, horrid, sticky, stinking mud. It was nothing like the red dirt from home. The weather was foul. It rained incessantly, and there was often heavy dew in the mornings. Then there was the fog. Everything was wet. His clothes were damp right through to his skin.

Brig. Gen. Victor Odlum, playing badminton with staff members near Lens.

If the weather and mud were the only things he had to contend with, he wouldn't have been quite so miserable. The rats and lice made every day a living hell. He was able to catch and kill the rats once in a while but there was no relief from the lice, from the endless biting and the scratching. The vermin hid in the seams of clothing and laid eggs that hatched by the thousands. No amount of washing — body or clothes —could get rid of them for long.

But, of course, the living conditions were not the worst aspects of war. At home friendships lasted a lifetime. In the trenches they could be over in seconds.

As the first cruel weeks dragged by, Chrystie lost his illusions about the glory of war. Perhaps the rudest awakening came when he realized that the stranger running towards him firing bullets really intended to kill him. An even more sobering realization was that he would have to kill the stranger first if he wanted to survive.

Laying a barbed-wire entanglement in a ditch, to slow any attackers.

Young Chrystie saw his share of action but, like every other soldier, he had to endure long hours just waiting for something to happen. The men had to remain ready, and most stayed close to the guns, but small groups would be assigned work duty replacing sections of the barbed wire barricades. They also had to dig new pits — and new graves.

The men who were not on duty would play cards or kill rats. Someone might open up a care package from home or read his letters out loud. To ward off the ever-present dampness, they would often light a fire in a helmet and make coffee or hot chocolate. Almost every afternoon as the darkness crept over the landscape, the sound of a harmonica would drift on the wind. It may have been

Briefly relieved from the trenches and off duty, soldiers of the Black Watch take in a regimental sports day, There are even civillians.

therapeutic for the player, but the lonely sound would set men's minds on home.

The men longed for a real bed, in a real room, in a real house — even a shack or a tent — to sleep in. But while on their 140-day assignments to the front, the trenches were their only home. Each man would keep track of the days and look forward to the long trek back to base camp where there would be showers, beds and a break from the elements. Then, all too soon, it was back to the front and back to life in the trenches for another 140 days.

By the time the war ended in 1918, Chrystie had had his fill of war. He was one of the lucky ones. He and his brothers came home relatively unscathed.

Chrystie Jenkins had left Prince Edward Island a boy. When he disembarked in December 1918 from the H.M.C.S. *Mauritania* at Halifax's Pier 21, he was a man and a seasoned soldier.

It had been a long two years and Chrystie had not found the glory and honour he had dreamed about. Instead, he had found more than enough blood, death, rats and mud to last a lifetime. After all he had seen and experienced, he was glad the army had made him wait a year.

When Chrystie came home to the island, he brought with him more than memories he'd rather forget. He brought a keepsake.

During one of the battles in France, Chrystie was hit in the chest by a piece of hot shrapnel. Thinking he was mortally wounded, he grabbed at the gaping hole in the front of his uniform only to find the shrapnel firmly embedded in the small New Testament he always carried in his front pocket. If it hadn't been for the Bible, the shrapnel would have pierced his heart.

When Chrystie showed his family the hole in the small book, he told them he had been saved by the Word of God.

Chrystie married a few years after the war and raised his family on Prince Edward Island. His descendents still have the shrapnel-ravaged New Testament and love to tell the story of how it had given this young Canadian soldier his second chance at life.

Chapter 2
THE DANGER TREE

Folklore is filled with stories of bravery, glory and war. Perhaps it was the false hope of glory that wooed the men of Newfoundland and Labrador from their rough and craggy shores in 1914 to the blood-wet earth near the small village of Beaumont Hamel.

During the Great War, almost half the male population of Newfoundland and Labrador enlisted. One tenth of them never returned home. Of those Newfoundlanders who perished at the Battle of the Somme, one of the last living things they saw was the Danger Tree.

The Danger Tree became a legend, and its story is still told today.

No-man's-land, situated between the Allied and German lines, was at one time a beautiful apple orchard. Most of these trees, however, had been destroyed by shelling, the axe and

Life in the trenches. One soldier keeps watch while three of his comrades sleep. Or are there four? July 1916, Battle of the Somme.

the digging of miles of trenches. One tree on the Allies' side of no-man's-land seemed impervious to man's destructive nature and stood tall, albeit void of life. It was as if the tree was standing in defiance against the enemy on the very edge of a shell hole.

The Newfoundlanders, one of four battalions of the British 29th Division's 88th Brigade, were new arrivals to the 60 miles of trenches along the Somme River. Their orders were to take up position close to the village, then go over the top, cut through their own rolls of barbed wire, sprint across no-man's-land, cut through the Germans' barbed wire and take out the enemy. Once the wire was cut the other forces would follow in waves. The assault was part of a plan to cut an access route clear through to the English Channel for the cavalry.

Empty shell casings after a bombardment. The explosive warheads have been fired over to the German lines.

From the wet and dubious safety of their trench, the Newfoundlanders surveyed the ground before them. The damp air smelled of spent explosives, latrines and another smell — more human, more basic, reminiscent of a butcher shop. It had rained for days, and the quagmire of boot-gripping mud pocked with shell craters stood between them and the rolls of wire they were to cut. The only relief in sight was the lone tree. The soldiers named it the Danger Tree and whispers soon travelled down the line: "Focus on the tree. If we can make it to the Danger Tree we'll be okay."

The men were a rag-tag mix of veterans from the battle at Suvla Bay, Gallipoli and a few new recruits — some of whom weren't old enough to shave, having lied about their age in order to enlist.

The night before the offensive, the boom of guns in the distance filled the air. The barrage of shelling had been going on for days. A line of flame and thunder stretched for

The Battle of Courcelette, *by painter Louis Weirter, 1918, shows the wild chaos of battle, and something new — tanks (left foreground).*

90 miles from Ypres to the Somme River. Some of the French townspeople, 30 miles away, sat in darkness on their roofs watching with morbid fascination the roaring shell flashes on the eastern skyline.

In the trenches, the men tried to ignore the barrage. The tunnels were deep — some with roofs and large enough to hold a battalion and a half. The men were safe as long as they stayed there undetected. But to move in or out of the trenches was death. Many were picked off by German sharpshooters.

Shelling had turned the once-solid lines of tunnels and trenches into a sea of craters. These craters were manned and defended. This duty was particularly dangerous as the cover was limited. Many times the men holding them were blown to pieces. Their replacements had to move the mangled human remains to one side before they could defend the line.

Safe or not, the mounting anxiety of being deep in the trenches and tunnels with the pounding of shells all around wore on the nerves of the most courageous. Sleep was impossible. As the newly arrived men from Newfoundland waited for their orders, some wrote letters home to their families, describing the horror of those hours of waiting.

The wasteland landmark. Around this point, bodies piled up in heaps.

As night gave over to morning, the ceaseless crashing "drum-fire" on both sides intensified. The barrage was one long, loud roar that deafened their ears and filled their souls with dread. The earth shook beneath their boots. Water lapped at their bodies. Dirt crumbled off the sides of the trenches. And still they waited.

The British had been pounding the German lines all week — mainly as a diversion to mask the noise of tunnelling that was going on. The 252 Tunnelling Company of the Royal Engineers had mined their way under an enemy stronghold on Hawthorn Ridge. They laid 45,000 pounds of dynamite with orders to blow the ridge at 3:30 a.m. But the detonation was postponed until later in the morning, a delay that played a tragic role in the disaster to follow.

Shortly after 7 a.m. the bombardment decreased, and half an hour later there came a huge underground explosion as the British blew the ridge. The sides of the trenches

*Blowing the Hawthorn Ridge mine. A British regiment was supposed
to rush to the lip of the crater, but the Germans got there first.*

shook and the men, standing ready, jumped with the
unexpected force of it. The sky filled with dust, smoke and
raining dirt. The plan failed, as the Germans reclaimed the
ridge before the dust had settled and the huge crater left
by the blast provided them with better cover than they had
when the ridge had been intact. The Allies were heading
into a death trap.

Whistles blew.

The South Wales Borderers went over the top first, yelling
as they charged at the double rows of barbed wire into a wall
of bullets. Men were cut in half by machine-gun fire, but some
managed to cut holes in the wire for the next wave. The holes
were narrow, only wide enough for one man to pass through at
a time. Bodies piled up and blocked the holes as the men were
shot down where they stood.

Those who made it through to no-man's-land charged
across the open field right into a crossfire that mowed down

man after man. No one reached their appointed talisman, the Danger Tree.

The Newfoundlanders were supposed to advance an hour after the Borderers had taken out the front line, with the 1st Battalion, Essex Regiment on their flank. They waited for the word, crouched and silent in the din around them. Guns chattered, men screamed, salvos shook the earth and still they waited. The word came through over the wire: the first wave had been unsuccessful, and the Germans were unmoved.

Then came the order: "Advance!" It reached the Newfoundlanders but not the 1st Essex. The Newfoundlanders were on their own.

Over the top the first group scrambled, down a slight slope and over the rows of trenches the Borderers had recently vacated. Climbing over bodies jammed in the narrow holes in the barbed wire, man after man zigzagged through, only to be met with the chattering fire of the German guns. Ahead of them lay half a mile of exposed land where not one soul was left alive. "C" and "D" companies of the Newfoundlanders followed at an interval of 100 yards.

Although bodies were piling up at the narrow channels through the wire, it at first seemed the advance was proceeding successfully. The soldiers moved half crouched, rifles loaded and ready. They hurled their grenades as fast as they could pull the pins and pumped bullets blindly into the German lines as they advanced. Falling into shell craters for cover, they would take a couple of breaths and then dash to the next hole. Around them the din continued, augmented now with screams, moans and the stench of fresh blood and burned cordite. Officers urged the soldiers on, through red-hot chunks of flying steel and flying dirt from the shelling. Bullets played a hellish tattoo on the metal wire and puffed the dirt around the men's feet. Exploding shells splattered body parts and rained blood and dirt around their heads. The wounded writhed at the feet of the next advancing wave, grabbing at their legs and pleading pitifully for help. The standing couldn't pause to help. They had to push onwards into the frantic mêlée ahead, concentrating only on the first step of their journey — the Danger Tree standing gnarled and bent against the horizon.

The regiment's numbers diminished at each of the four tangled rows of wire. Almost no one in the first advance made it past them. Smoke filled the air and blurred their vision, thundering explosions filled their ears and each man was an island unto himself, alone in a sea of struggling humanity.

"I have to make that tree. I'll be okay if I can only make that tree," many of them thought. For some it was their last thought as bullets found them, smashing and ripping into their flesh. Stunned, others gasped for breath, watching in horror as their life's blood pumped out of them and pooled on the muddy earth at their feet. Some tried to crawl back for help, others tried to save themselves, crouched bleeding in shell craters to bandage their own mortal wounds in vain, or to stuff intestines back into their bellies. Men in manic states charged the enemy without weapons, or stood their ground when their ammunition ran out and cursed the Germans in their dying moment. The enemy kept shooting and the barrage of shells created a wall of flames hotter and more terrifying than hell itself. They were so close, only a few yards away from the German guns.

Opening and dedicating the Newfoundland Memorial Park at Beaumont Hamel Park, France, on June 7, 1925.

Still, the men of the Newfoundland Regiment kept coming. They fought as a unit, but each man met death alone. In less than 30 minutes and at the cost of hundreds of lives, this part of the Battle of the Somme was over for the brave men from Newfoundland.

When the roll was called the next morning, Sunday, July 2, 1916, out of the original 801 men, only 68 could answer "here!"

In the shadow of the Danger Tree, the other 733 men of the Newfoundland Regiment had been killed or wounded. Many were buried where they had fallen and the Danger Tree became their headstone.

Another world war and many years have passed since the Battle of the Somme. Today, in France, there is a bronze statue of a Newfoundland stag caribou. He stands defiantly facing the enemy lines as a memorial to the men from Newfoundland and Labrador who lost their lives on

The caribou memorial statue in Beaumont Hamel park.

the first day of the Battle of the Somme. The Danger Tree also, preserved with cement at its base, still stands.

A portion of the inscription on the Beaumont Hamel memorial plaque reads:

Those who got farthest reached the barb wire lines
Where they were cut down in the narrow gaps
Which intelligence had thought would be much wider,
Through which 'slits' stormed shot and shell and enfilade
Through holes so poorly blown that the men must go single file,
Must wait in line as if waiting for breakfast.
Never was there such exposure so naked,
Bodies piled up to a point, where it broke the wire
Killed instantly by machine gun fire in the death traps;
Yet many of the wounded helped clear a path
For buddies pressing forward through the drift,
Their cry with that spirit "Right into it boys!"
Spoken by men who by now could speak only to the sod:
These were the Men of the Caribou, flagged red, white and blue.
Gone in the same time it took to eat breakfast: Gone.

Chapter 3
COMRADE IN WHITE

Thomas Arthur Cramer was born on August 21, 1895, the eldest of ten boys and one girl.

At the outbreak of the war in 1914, Arthur, as his family called him, felt it was his duty to fight. So, on January 3, 1916 he left his parents' farm in Baldur, Manitoba and went to Winnipeg to sign up with the Canadian Expeditionary Force (C.E.F.).

By October 26, 1917 he had finished his training in England and was sent to Belgium with the 3rd Canadian Division of the 46th Infantry Battalion, part of the South Saskatchewan Regiment. He and his fellow soldiers arrived in Belgium and began their march to Passchendaele Ridge in the area best known as Ypres. Arthur's battalion was part of a 20,000 man force — all Canadians.

Arthur had a very bad feeling about going into battle. It would be his first taste of real combat, so naturally he was

Tired Canadians returning to base camp in November 1916. Those steel helmets were a recent issue, that saved many lives.

apprehensive. He knew the Allies were facing a stiff fight. There had already been one battle for this small strip of land. The first had been a bloody mess with many casualties on both sides. There was no reason to believe this battle would be any less bloody.

As he and the rest of the battalion were marching along the road to the front, they passed a line of men returning to base camp from Ypres. They looked exhausted, their eyes glazed with dark circles around them. They stared straight ahead with vacant expressions. The wounded were wrapped in dirty bandages, and some hobbled along on crutches. Those fit enough to walk unaided took turns helping their less fortunate buddies or carried stretchers bearing the severely wounded.

Some wounded men walk back after a battle, some can only lie and wait. A transport is broken. Stretchers pile up. Shells are landing.

Occasionally, a truck passed by the line and honked its horn. The men looked neither right nor left. They simply moved over to let the vehicle pass and continued walking.

Arthur swallowed and tried neither to stare nor to think of what lay ahead. He wondered if he would look like these hollow-eyed men after his 140 days at the front, or even if he would live to tell the story. He felt sick. He tried not to think of his family, but it was hard not to.

With eyes forward, Arthur squared his shoulders and marched on. After a few minutes, he became aware of a man moving among the oncoming soldiers. He seemed out of place among the bedraggled men in their torn and mud-splashed uniforms. He was dressed all in white and was spotlessly clean.

Arthur was struck by his compassionate face and watched as the man reached out to some of the wounded. Arthur thought he must be a minister or a chaplain.

Some of the soldiers he touched ignored the man in white. Others reached out and touched his hands, smiling, wanting him to stay with them. Even some of the men on stretchers who looked like they were struggling for their next breath reached out and grasped his hands. The man smiled in return as he took their hands.

Arthur wondered who he was.

He dropped his gaze as he drew abreast of the stranger. There was something about the man that made him uncomfortable. He didn't feel threatened exactly, but he felt something wasn't right and he didn't want to look into the man's eyes. He couldn't. No, he couldn't acknowledge him in any way. He was suddenly very afraid.

After the man had passed by, Arthur was left with a hollow feeling inside. He didn't know why, but he knew he'd be seeing the man again.

When he arrived at the front, Arthur's heart sank. He knew he would be fighting in a quagmire, but this was worse than anything he had ever imagined. He climbed wearily into the trenches and dug himself a sleeping cave. It was not easy digging into the sticky, oozing mud while standing in a foot of filthy, slushy water. As Arthur watched the rats swimming in the bottom of the trench he wondered, not for the first time, why he had signed up.

He crawled into his sleeping cave, trying not to think of it as a grave, and closed his eyes. It was impossible to sleep. The fighting had abated, and there wasn't even a sound to

The mud, the mud, the mud. They fought in a quagmire. Soldiers often had to walk on duckboards to cross flooded shell holes.

suggest there was an enemy out there. In the dark he listened intently to the silence. He was unnerved by the thought that the silence was listening to him. His mind wandered across no-man's-land. Out there, across that empty field of barbed wire, was a German lying in a dirt hole similar to his, who was thinking about killing him tomorrow. An icy shiver passed through his body and goosebumps rippled down his arms.

Arthur rolled over and tried to shut out the sounds of the ever-present rats. They loved the darkness, and spent the night racing through the trenches chewing whatever they could find. The men who had been there a while didn't even move when the squealing rodents scampered over them. They snored and slept soundly. Arthur and the other raw recruits jumped, yelled and threw things at the loathsome creatures, but it didn't help.

As much as Arthur despised the rats, he hated the dampness even more. He couldn't stand the feeling of being wet all the time. Even in his sleeping roll, the dampness had permeated every layer of clothing he wore. His feet felt clammy and cold. He longed for hot water and clean socks.

Arthur's musings of clean, dry clothes were shattered by the sound of a single gunshot. A jumpy sentry, thinking he had heard something, had loosed off a round into the night. There was no return fire. As the echo died, the tense silence enveloped the men again. Arthur almost wished for more gunfire — at least he'd feel less alone.

He turned over again and his thoughts turned to home and the days when shooting meant bagging game, not blowing a man's head off. He had learned to shoot as soon as he was old enough to hold a gun. He had started with rabbits and gophers, then went on to bigger game. He remembered the first time his father had taken him on a real hunting trip. He had felt so grown up and figured he was finally a man in his father's eyes.

Then they came across a deer in a big thicket of poplars. The big buck stood tall and proud and Arthur slowly and silently raised his gun and took aim. He saw the animal give a shiver that trembled down its flank, almost as if it sensed that death was near. Arthur held his breath and kept the stock steady as he squeezed the trigger.

The gun recoiled as the bullet exploded out of the muzzle. The deer sprang forward and then dropped to the ground in mid-jump. It was a perfect headshot!

Arthur and his father, Matthew, ran to their prize. The deer was still warm and quivering. Matthew was grinning from ear to ear as he slapped his boy on the back. Young Arthur looked down at the deer, and a mixture of emotions swept over him. He had killed to put meat on the table, and he

Some Canadians, in their little mud homes in the trench: their "sleeping holes."

knew he should be proud. But he had killed a beautiful and graceful living creature. His pride was tinged with sadness.

Arthur lay in his dirt hole in that foreign land and wondered how he would feel when he shot and killed his first man.

Along with the other men, Arthur was woken before daybreak. The usual stand-to was changed as orders came down for an attack. As directed, he and his comrades climbed to the edge of the parapet. They had been ordered to fall into positions for a united push against the enemy. They were to start with a barrage of fire to cover the artillery while it was moving forward. Once the artillery was in place, the men were to move out and gain as much ground as possible.

It wasn't going to be an easy battle. The last big push had resulted in 13,000 casualties. Arthur knew this one would cost the Allies at least that many men, probably more. Across no-man's-land the Germans were ready and waiting.

While the Canadians waited for the signal, a hush fell over the trenches. Arthur realized that even the birds had stopped singing, and though he felt a breeze, the trees were still. It made the hair on the back of his neck prickle and his stomach tightened into a knot. He tried not to think and tried not to analyse his feelings of doom. He tried only to focus on waiting for the signal to go over the top and break through the enemy lines.

The pause lasted so long that Arthur began to lose his concentration. He felt he wasn't alone. Of course he wasn't alone — there were men beside him on either side and thousands more all down the line. But this was a different feeling, as if someone was standing behind him, staring, waiting for him to turn around. His skin prickled and then he felt a touch on his shoulder as light as a feather. His heart leapt as he slowly looked around and saw a man standing off to one side. It wasn't a fellow soldier. It was the man in white.

Arthur's first instinct was to shout a warning and level his rifle at the intruder, but one look from the stranger stopped him. The man in white was smiling, and there was no escaping those eyes and that compassionate smile. A feeling of well-being emanated from the man and Arthur instantly felt at peace. He knew that whatever happened in the coming battle, he would still be at peace.

The man in white moved away, and Arthur watched as he slowly drifted down the line. Now and again the stranger put his hand out to touch the shoulder of a soldier standing at the ready. Most of the soldiers turned and looked. Some smiled and nodded. Others looked confused and surprised.

The man continued to move along the trench in this way until he rounded the corner and was gone from view. Arthur watched him as he disappeared and realized that he was no longer afraid. He was ready to face the enemy.

Arthur looked out over the parapet again and calmly waited for the order to go over the top. The order never came. The artillery was stuck in the mud, so the attack was delayed.

Glad of the respite, Arthur leaned against the dirt wall of the trench and scribbled a note to his mother back in Baldur. He told her about the man in white and explained that although he wasn't sure what it meant, he knew he would be fine. He told her not to worry about him; he would always be with her. He folded the note neatly and put it into his helmet.

Moments later, a shell landed in the trench at Passchendaele where Thomas Arthur Cramer stood. He died instantly without knowing what had hit him and without ever firing a shot. The fighting started a few moments later and, before the battle was done, more than 15,000 men were dead.

Three weeks later, Arthur's mother received a telegram informing her of her son's death. Along with the telegram she read his last words: the hastily written note that described the man in white. Arthur's family were distraught. His body was buried near the battlefield, so there was no funeral. All they had was a memorial service without a body, attended by neighbours and friends thousands of miles from the spot where their precious son lay.

Six months later, the Cramers were dealt another blow. On May 3, 1918, one of the younger boys joined up.

Delbert, who was born on November 13, 1896, was only a year younger than Arthur. He felt his brother's death deeply

Dawn on the day of the Battle of Passchendaele. This dramatic (and possibly enhanced) photo was taken near Zonnebeke Station.

and knew he had to go overseas to see where Arthur had died. He wanted to say goodbye, and he wanted to fight the enemy that had taken his brother's life.

His mother said she understood, but she cried bitterly when he left. His father shook Delbert's hand and told him that, no matter what happened, he would always be proud of him and Arthur.

Men of the Royal Canadian Artillery wait for a steam tractor to be unstuck from the mud, so it can pull their gun into position.

When peace was declared on November 11, 1918, the Cramer family breathed a sigh of relief. Delbert was still in training at Camp Hughes, and with the war over, they expected him home any day. They must have been bitterly disappointed when they got his next letter.

Delbert wrote in December to tell them he was being sent overseas as part of the transitional army. There was a great deal of rebuilding to be done and peacekeeping troops were still needed. He was due to ship out in May 1919.

The evening of April 12, 1919 was cold and bleak on the prairie. The rest of the country was looking forward to spring, but in Baldur the snow was still deep and the nights crisp and clear.

Matthew Cramer was restless. He went to bed early and tried to sleep, but he kept thinking of the day he had said goodbye to Delbert at the station. He had not been able to shake off the feeling he would never see his boy again. He tried to tell himself he was having these misgivings because they had lost Arthur. But no matter what he told himself, he still felt the same.

Finally, at three in the morning, he drifted off to sleep. But he did not sleep for long. Violent dreams haunted him and he awoke feverish and soaked in sweat. He gave up trying to sleep and decided to get up and take a ride before sunrise. Quietly, so as not to disturb his wife, he got dressed and went to the barn.

Comforted by the warmth of the barn and the smell of horses, Matthew relaxed a little. His horse snorted a greeting while Matthew saddled him then led him out into the morning air.

Matthew loved his horses and was proud of the home he had made in Baldur. His family was thriving, and although the country was groaning under the burden of financial stress, his family didn't want for much. Running a farm was hard work but he enjoyed the lifestyle and he hoped his sons would follow in his footsteps.

Letting the horse take the lead, Matthew looked up at the waning moon and the lightening horizon. In the distance he could see the crossroad at Playfair Corners and the cemetery beyond. He gazed at the familiar landscape briefly and was about to turn away when his eyes were drawn back to the cemetery.

He stood up in his stirrups to get a better look. The cemetery was glowing. It was as though a hundred candles had been placed on the gravestones. His heart was pounding.

Sleep when you can. Canadians in a front-line trench. Being below ground level would protect you — except from a direct hit.

He was torn between investigating and turning the horse around and galloping for home, but his curiosity won.

As he drew near the crossroads he pulled back on the reins, bringing his horse to a standstill. He could see into the graveyard now and he couldn't believe his eyes. Drifting soundlessly, as if his feet weren't touching the ground, was a man dressed in white. The glow was emanating from the figure. Even Matthew's horse stared. Matthew could feel the beast shiver, so he stroked the horse's neck to reassure him.

The man didn't seem to see or hear Matthew. He simply drifted between the crosses and grave markers as if he were looking for something. Then he stopped and Matthew shivered with dread. The man was looking at the row that had been designated for the Cramer family.

The man knelt and gently placed his hand on the soil. Then he looked over his shoulder, directly at Matthew. With a sad smile on his face, the man, still kneeling, slowly faded away.

Matthew bowed his head and sobbed. He knew his son Delbert was dead.

The telegram came a week later. Delbert had died on April 12, 1919 — the night Matthew had seen the man in white. The young soldier had not even left Canada. His death had been caused by an adverse reaction to an inoculation. Delbert was 22 years old, the same age as Arthur when he had died.

Delbert Morden Cramer was buried in the Baldur Cemetery in the exact place where Matthew had seen the Comrade in White place his hand.

Chapter 4
RITA SIMPSON'S STORY

Rita Simpson was alone in the cold Winnipeg winter of 1917. Her husband, Edgar, was somewhere in France fighting with the Canadian Expeditionary Force. She wasn't sure exactly where he was. She knew only that he was at the front.

Rita looked forward to Edgar's letters and read them over and over until she had memorized every word. She lovingly placed each one back in its envelope and added it to the stack she kept in her keepsake box.

Edgar's letters were sporadic, and sometimes she went weeks without hearing from him. Rita always combed the lists of missing troops in the newspaper and was flooded with relief when she couldn't find his name. Then, she became frustrated because she hadn't heard from him. She knew that Edgar wrote to her every day and saved the letters until he could mail

Soldiers knee-deep in mud in a shallow trench. Since they are carrying shovels, they may have been ordered to make the trench deeper.

them out. She cried every time she received the longed-for stack and realized anew how much he loved her.

She often sat cross-legged on the living room floor, organizing them according to date and reading them in order from start to finish. Then she would read them once more, make herself some tea and start at the beginning again.

Every night before going to bed, Rita prayed for her husband and begged God to send him home. Living without him was agony, and she didn't want to think of what the rest of her life would be like if he did not return.

For some reason today, September 4, was especially difficult for her. She was restless and couldn't concentrate on anything. She knew Edgar was in danger every minute of every day and was living in the most dreadful conditions

The St. Julien battlefield.

imaginable, but today she was feeling sorry for herself. She missed him and felt so very alone.

Not wanting to stay in and brood, Rita went to her "wife's group," a number of military wives who met in the afternoons and knitted and sewed items for the boys overseas. She was comforted by the thought that perhaps something she made would find its way to her husband.

She felt desperately in need of support that day, and was glad the others were in a talkative mood. They shared stories about the first time they had met their husbands and funny things that had happened through the years.

Rita and Edgar hadn't been married long, so the others teased her about still being in the honeymoon stage. Rita didn't mind the teasing. It made her laugh, and there weren't too many things that could do that.

She, in turn, told the others how she and Edgar had met.

A Canadian narrow-gauge gasoline-engined locomotive pulls three gondola cars loaded with shells through a shattered village.

It had been at a social, and he had walked all the way across the hall to ask her to dance. She smiled as she told her friends how handsome he looked — and how nervous he was.

She had pretended she wasn't watching him as he made his way over to her, but her air of indifference dissolved when he touched her shoulder. A tremor ran right through her body. She was so startled by the feeling that she looked up into his eyes. She knew then — they would be together forever.

Rita felt better after reminiscing and laughing, but by the time she got home she felt more bereft than ever. That evening she knelt by her bed and asked God to send her love to Edgar, wherever he might be. She wanted him to know how much she missed him and how very much she loved him. Her sleep was fitful. She tossed and turned and dreamed strange and confusing dreams. Finally, she decided to get up and make herself a cup of tea. She was about to get out of bed when

Canadians in a well-made trench, polishing bullets. Dirty bullets were more likely to jam in a rifle or machine gun, making it useless.

she froze. Edgar was walking in through the open door of her bedroom. Rita's hand flew to her mouth and she gave a cry of joy.

He was still in his infantry uniform, which didn't really surprise her at first, until she realized that it was filthy and there was mud on his boots. She held her breath when she looked into his face. His eyes, although smiling and full of love, seemed distant.

Her heart started beating erratically as she realized her husband wasn't really there in her room. It was a dream, a vision or simply her imagination. All the joy drained out of her and she began sobbing. As if to comfort her, Edgar took off his helmet and laid it on the bed next to her foot. She felt the weight of the helmet on the mattress and saw the blankets depress around it. Her eyes flew to her husband's face. If she was seeing him only in her imagination, the helmet was imaginary too. Yet it looked and felt real. Could it be that Edgar was also real?

By now her heart was throbbing wildly and her mouth was dry. She wanted him to be there with every fibre of her being. She held out her hand to him.

Edgar opened his mouth as if to speak, but there was no sound. Rita started to panic. She had read somewhere that ghosts were not allowed to speak. She reached out for him imploringly.

He took a step back from the bed and smiled, mouthing the words, "I love you." Then he turned and walked towards the wall, fading away before he reached it.

The helmet, still on the bed beside her foot, also faded.

Dazed, Rita reached down to the foot of her bed. The indent from the helmet was still there. She placed her hand into the depression and started to cry with dry, racking sobs. She knew her husband was dead. He had come to say goodbye.

Weeks later the official telegram came, delivered by a sombre looking youth in an army uniform. Along with the notice of her husband's death was a dirty, ragged envelope containing Edgar's last letter. It was short. He simply told her that he loved her, that he'd always be with her, and that he knew — no matter what happened — that he would see her again.

The telegram stated that these were Edgar's last words, written moments before the battle that ended his life. The letter had been found inside his helmet.

Rita Simpson told this story to her family many times over the years. They found it so moving that it passed into family legend, handed down from generation to generation. Edgar Simpson was killed on September 4, 1917 during the Third Battle of Ypres. He is buried in Ypres Memorial Cemetery.

Chapter 5
BILLY BISHOP VERSUS THE RED BARON

Sooner or later Canadian flying ace Billy Bishop would come face to face with his nemesis, the Red Baron, and they would clash in the sky over a field in France. People on both sides of the war followed the movements of both aces, and those who liked to bet laid down their money. It was only a matter of time.

These two flying aces had become the subject of exaggerated stories that were told and retold across Canada and Britain. The real story, stripped of sensationalism, is still amazing.

The "Red Baron" was, of course, a nickname, but it was not the only nickname the German flying ace had collected. The French called him "le petit rouge" (the little red) and his countrymen called their hero "der rote Kampfflieger" (the Red Battle-Flyer). The word "red" was part of every name because that was the colour the Baron and his men painted their planes. This helped them to identify each other in the heat of

William Avery "Billy" Bishop in the cockpit of his Nieuport 17 fighter.
The Nieuport's weapon is the single Lewis gun above Bishop's head.

the battle and at the same time let the enemy know that the infamous Red Baron or one of his men was hot on their trail. As his reputation grew, the sight of a red biplane struck terror into the hearts of Germany's enemies.

The Baron's real name was Manfred Von Richthofen. He was born on May 2, 1892 in Breslau, Germany to Major Albrecht Von Richthofen, a Prussian nobleman, and his wife Kunigunde. The name Richthofen means "court of judgement," a fact that was not overlooked when he gained his reputation as the Red Baron.

Von Richthofen was the firstborn son of four children. He had one sister, Ilse, and two younger brothers. As a young man he wasn't interested or proficient in books or figures, preferring instead to play sports and ride horses. He loved to compete and he loved to win — which he did most of the time. He dreamed of becoming a cavalry officer, so after graduating from grade school, Von Richthofen attended the Royal Military Academy at Lichterfelde. He was 22 years old and still a student at the academy when World War I broke out.

While Billy Bishop's background was very different from that of his adversary, the two men were similar in several ways.

William (Billy) Avery Bishop was born on February

Germany's deadly Baron Captain Manfred Von Richthofen.

8, 1894 in Owen Sound, Ontario to William Avery Bishop Sr. and his wife Margaret Louise Greene. The third of four children, he was named after his father. His oldest brother had died in infancy before Billy was born. He had another older brother, Worth, and a younger sister, Louise.

Young Billy Bishop was an indifferent student and books couldn't seem to hold his attention for very long. Billy wasn't tall — not quite 5' 7" — and had a fair complexion, light brown hair and blue eyes. He enjoyed action, yet he didn't enjoy team sports. While hockey was a favourite pastime for most boys in the area, Bishop didn't like standing around while others were making the action.

This was fine for the most part, but occasionally it landed him in difficult situations.

As a boy in Owen Sound, Ontario, Bishop was inspired by the AEA Silver Dart, the first powered airplane to fly in Canada.

For example, Billy Bishop read a series of newspaper articles about John McCurdy, a pilot who had managed to lift off the frozen surface of Baddeck Lake in Nova Scotia in the Silver Dart on February 23, 1909. Bishop was 15 years old at the time, and while he hated schoolwork and reading, he loved the idea of flying and couldn't read enough about this aeroplane. He was convinced he could build a better machine and fly it farther than the third of a mile that McCurdy had managed. With newspaper pictures of the plane in hand, he started building his masterpiece in the barn.

He nailed boards together and attached an orange crate and cardboard in the middle to form his cockpit. He had to improvise. He draped the whole structure with a couple of bed sheets, tying them to the frame with string, since he didn't have canvas or glue. He dragged the contraption to the roof of the house, jumped in, careened off the shingles and nose-dived straight into the ground. His sister Louise witnessed the incident and helped dig him out of the wreckage. Besides hurt pride he sustained a long gash on the inside of his leg, resulting in a lifelong scar.

While his older brother, Ward, did well in school and earned top marks, Billy Bishop was continually in trouble for fighting, from which he never backed down. Bishop's inability to apply himself to schoolwork concerned his parents, especially his lawyer father. However, none of his parents' or teachers' efforts helped the young man to focus.

Bishop's father thought that his son needed a challenge to occupy his mind. So for Christmas one year, William Sr. gave him a .22 calibre rifle and promised to pay him 25 cents for every squirrel he shot. Squirrels are fast and hard to shoot. William Sr. hoped that the concentration needed for shooting squirrels would also be good for Billy.

Much to his parents' surprise, Bishop rose to the challenge and was soon bagging a squirrel with every bullet. His father was very impressed. Bishop had another surprise for his parents: this enterprising young man had developed a thriving business — squirrel removal at 25 cents per animal. He was so successful in ridding Owen Sound of the pesky rodents that the *Sun* newspaper dubbed him "the Pied Piper of Owen Sound."

His reputation for shooting soon spread and his friends often joked that Bishop could shoot the head off a fly at a full gallop.

Like his future nemesis, Von Richthofen, Bishop loved riding and wanted a career in the cavalry. In 1911, at the age of 17, he was accepted into the Royal Military College of Canada, located in Kingston, Ontario. Riding horses at home was fun, but at the college it was too much like work — he had to clean the stalls, curry and care for them as well as ride them. One day while out on a training exercise he saw a small silver plane land on a field. His interest in flying was revived.

Unfortunately for Billy his school troubles followed him to the Military College. He was set back a year due to alleged cheating in his first-year exams.

Bishop was 20 when war was declared in 1914. The outbreak of war interrupted life for both Bishop and Von Richthofen, but they were determined to do their duty. Finding the cavalry unromantic and impractical for frontline fighting, both men switched their focus and trained for the air force.

At first Billy Bishop was nervous and hesitant while flying. Horses responded well to body language; planes didn't. He stayed in the back of the formation rather than the front.

But Bishop had an advantage over other flyers in this war. He had joined up early and received a long and thorough training. His takeoffs and handling of the aircraft in the air showed great promise. However, landings challenged him. He crash landed more often than any other Canadian pilot. Fortunately, luck was with him — he walked away from every wreck, only suffering a slight injury to one knee during one of his landings. Eventually he built up his confidence and took to the skies with a proprietary air, seeming fearless, almost arrogant in the face of death.

When he had completed his training he was sent overseas and assigned to 60 Squadron at Filescamp Farm near Arras, France, flying the Nieuport 17 fighter. When Bishop arrived Manfred Von Richthofen and his flying circus were already widely known — and feared. Even though the Red Baron didn't know of Billy Bishop's existence, Bishop heard of the Baron almost as soon as he arrived.

The odds were stacked against Bishop ever becoming a legend in the Royal Flying Corps (RFC). The average lifespan of a rookie fighter pilot in the corps was only 11 days at the time of Bishop's arrival, a month that was dubbed "Bloody April." Many people didn't even give Bishop 11 days, partly due to his inability to land his plane in one piece.

William A. "Billy" Bishop as a cadet at Royal Military College in Kingston.

Shortly after being assigned to duty in England he crash landed his Nieuport 17 plane at the feet of his Commanding Officer (CO), Lieutenant W.M. Fry, who was less than pleased. Bishop walked away from the crash without a scratch, which was a miracle. The pilots at that time flew without parachutes, in flimsy planes made of wood and fabric. One spark and the aircraft would go up in flames within seconds. So, even though Bishop was fortunate enough yet again to walk away from this latest embarrassment, the plane was a write-off. The CO berated him for the loss, ending his tirade with an order for Billy Bishop to report back to flying school.

Seen from the trenches, airplanes seemed to offer a better, cleaner sort of war.

Bishop was heartbroken. He knew that if he returned to flying school he might miss the rest of the war and may never be permitted to fly again. Fortunately for him there was a keen shortage of pilots, and with pressure from the squadron leader who believed in Bishop's abilities, the CO recanted his order. Bishop again took to the skies.

The Royal Flying Corps faced a huge challenge. The German pilots were better trained, flew superior machines and used more advanced weapons. Daredevils like Bishop didn't usually last very long. Billy, however, was an excellent marksman.

On his first official flight out, March 25, 1917, Bishop took part in his first dogfight. Bringing up the rear of the formation he found himself watching as three German Albatros D-III biplanes dived at the tail of the Squadron Leader's plane and lined up for their shot. Major A.J.L. (Jack) Scott was crippled and could walk only with the aid of two canes, yet was still an active fighter. Even with his experience, Scott was having trouble shaking his pursuers, as he weaved back and forth to no avail. Acting on instinct and ignoring his own safety Bishop dove into the middle of the fight. He squeezed off a few rounds and peppered the fuselage of one of the German planes. The Albatros turned over and fell away in a spin. Bishop had been warned of this German ruse. The German flyers would often turn off their engines and fall into a spiral, feigning death. Close to the ground they would boot up their engines and pull out, to fight again another day.

Suspicious, Bishop followed his prey, the nose of his plane pointed towards the ground. As Bishop expected, the German pulled out of the dive well before hitting the earth. Bishop was right there waiting for him. Triumphantly, he landed on the German's tail with his guns blazing. He didn't let up until he saw smoke, and the German didn't stand a chance. The Albatros burst into flames and hit the ground in a puff of flames and smoke.

Bishop was elated. He had his first fight and his first kill.

He'd been so carried away with his chase that he didn't know where he was. He looked around to get his bearings. The fight had carried him deep into enemy territory and his engine had oiled up during the dive. It sputtered and died. Bishop turned towards British lines and glided as far as he could until he saw a place to touch down. As he lost altitude his plane was peppered with machine-gun fire from the ground and Bishop was sure he was about to become a prisoner of war. Gliding in effortlessly, he landed his plane safely in a small clearing.

Grabbing his Very pistol along with one cartridge, he ran from the plane and jumped into the nearest ditch, prepared to defend himself. Soldiers appeared and ran towards him. Bishop gripped his pistol and took aim — until he realized they were British.

The soldiers helped him hide his plane, and Bishop spent the night repairing the engine. In the morning, satisfied the machine would get him home, he taxied down the field preparing to take off. The field was damp and rough, and as his Nieuport gathered speed its propeller hit a rock and split in half. Bishop abandoned the plane and rejoined the British soldiers, spending the night in a trench until he could rejoin his squadron the next day by road.

Bishop was on his way up. Jack Scott promoted him to flight commander, and Bishop jumped into his assignment with vigour and very little forethought. Thinking he was invincible, he led his flight out twice without a proper plan and in the process lost four men. Those four deaths hit him very hard. Realizing that men had died as a result of his lack of planning and overconfidence he threw himself at the problem. While Billy hadn't enjoyed hockey as a boy he had since learned the importance of teamwork. Now he planned on his men playing a type of aerial hockey. Whoever made contact faked, passed or played. His teammates would pass the enemy planes back and forth between them, and when the time was right the one closest to the net — the target — made the shot. Bishop didn't care who made the kill, as long as all his players returned home. His men learned to trust him and the team became a force to be reckoned with.

He had three fights under his belt, and he planned to have more.

While Bishop was formulating his plans, the Baron was following the strategy he had been using successfully since the beginning of the war. Not surprisingly, he also

A Royal Aircraft Factory R.E.7, the first aircraft type in which Bishop flew into combat. He was in the back seat, as observer and gunner.

used sports tactics, but he planned his play very differently. Von Richthofen set up his men as though they were playing football. He ordered the play. The men blocked the other side and protected him so he could make the score. He lost a lot of men that way, but he scored the most kills and became the greatest and most skilful ace the Germans had.

When Von Richthofen looked back at his record, he was justifiably proud. In November 1916 he shot down British ace Major Lanoe Hawker, marking his 11th victory. By January 1917 — two months before Bishop's first official flight — he had been credited with 16 kills and named Germany's top ace. He was given command of the prestigious Jasta 11, an honour many German pilots vied for. The legend of the Red Baron had begun.

A modern replica of the Nieuport 17, in which Bishop gained most of his victories. Though it had only a single Lewis gun, it was agile.

Although Bishop was not yet a legend, he was well on his way. On April 7, 1917 he was awarded the Military Cross for shooting down an observation balloon and the Albatros that had tried to protect it. The next day he attacked a formation of six German Albatroses, knocking three of them out of the sky and watching gleefully as the others limped home. By the end of April, after only five weeks at the front, Bishop had made 17 kills. He became the squadron's top ace. Soon the German's nicknamed him "Hell's Handmaiden."

The Baron was now aware of the crazy Canadian and anticipated meeting him in combat. Bishop was eager to meet the Baron, too. Each combed the skies for a glimpse of the other every time their planes took to the air. Every once in a while they would catch sight of each other in the sky, but the opportunity to face off never arose. While both looked forward to the fight, they remained patient. It was simply a matter of time and of timing.

They finally met on the last day of April 1917. At 9 a.m. the men of Bishop's "C" Flight took to the air in their Nieuport planes on a hunt for Germans. After an uneventful mission, they headed for home to refuel. They crossed the front line and climbed to 13,000 feet, where they were out of range of the ground artillery. Constantly on the lookout for the enemy they watched the sun for the unexpected. Fighters would often try to attack from above with the sun behind them, using the glare as a shield.

As Bishop's squadron reached the skies above Douai they could see the Baron's group of red Albatroses below them. Bishop wagged his wings, letting his men know the battle was on. He went into a straight dive and another of the Nieuports plummeted towards the ground along with him. The duo had dived from out of the sun. Bishop was excited — his hands trembled and were wet with sweat. This was the battle he had been waiting for. But he was so eager to meet the Baron that he overshot the enemy planes, losing the element of surprise.

More German planes came out of nowhere and "C" Flight gave chase, leaving Bishop to deal with the Baron one on one. Manfred Von Richthofen was startled, but he recovered quickly, diving and banking to get into a better position. He usually had more backup but he felt he could take this little pup on his own. He locked his gaze on his adversary — his next kill.

Bishop knew he was an easy target for the Baron and his remaining two planes. He fumbled for his flare gun and signalled his men to come back into formation. They had their hands full, so were in no position to respond. Billy was on his own.

Bishop circled back up to a higher altitude and tried to figure out his best strategy. The Baron had disappeared, so

Bishop circled the area slowly, looking for his prey. As Bishop looked up he saw something in the air above him that made his heart leap: two German Gothas heading for England on a bombing run. He knew how much damage they could do, so even though he was on his own, and did not know whether the Baron was still looking for him, he decided to take a chance and go for the bombers. German fighters were always prime targets, but protecting England from the bombers took precedence. He banked, pulled up and climbed into position for the kill.

Bishop knew he had the upper hand. Even though the Gothas were well armed, they were slow and difficult to manoeuvre. Sliding under one of the planes, Bishop lined up for the shot. In the same instant the other Gotha opened fire on him. In the nick of time he dropped into a dive and swooped out of range of its guns. Lining up on the other side of the second plane, he fixed it in his sights. Bishop squeezed the trigger. Nothing — his gun was jammed. Swearing and battling with his gun, he looked up to see a German Albatros heading right for him.

The Baron had never let Bishop out of his sight. He had simply waited until his prey was distracted. Without waiting for the inevitable splatter of bullets, Bishop pointed his Nieuport straight down and plummeted towards the ground. Pulling up at the very last minute he applied full flaps, cut the throttle and made a rough landing in a field. The Baron's plane had followed, swooped up at the last minute and roared overhead.

Worried about his men and anxious to get back into the air to stop the bombers, Bishop let out a string of expletives at his gun. Getting a grip on himself, he began stripping it down and found the problem. Minutes later he was back in the air and searching for the Gothas.

The Baron circled the area and was soon joined by some of his men. He headed back towards the bombers, knowing instinctively that Bishop wouldn't have given up so easily.

Climbing high into the sky, Bishop searched the ground for aircraft shadows. He found them, and by following their rippling movement he soon found the Gothas. He revved his engine and

Group Captain A. J. L. Scott, Bishop's CO in 60 Squadron.

went in for the kill. He was closing in fast, his trigger finger itching, when he saw something out of the corner of his eye. The hair on the back of his neck stood on end. He glanced quickly over his right shoulder. Coming in fast on his tail he saw no less than six scarlet Albatros fighters. The Baron had judged his adversary well and he and his boys were closing in for the kill.

Bishop broke into a sweat. With the bombers below and the fighters above, he was surrounded. The red colour of the planes added to Bishop's anxiety. He was deathly afraid. The Baron was a killer and Bishop knew when he dropped the gauntlet his enemy would pick it up. Ignoring the churning in the pit of his stomach, Bishop pulled hard on the stick. His plane leapt straight up like an arrow shot from a bow. The Nieuport

The Germans were confident. So confident that ladies sometimes visited between sorties.

catapulted into the sky until forward momentum was lost, then slowed down. Waiting until he was almost at a standstill, Bishop held his breath and timed his next move.

The Nieuport started to shake and groan with the stress and still Bishop waited. Finally, after glancing below to see exactly where his targets were, he flipped sideways and started falling. Gunning the motor to full throttle Bishop aimed his plane at the German fighters. The Germans were taken by surprise and fired wildly while scrambling out of the way. Now that he had the upper hand, Bishop started playing with the enemy. He figured they needed a good game of chicken, Canadian style. Bishop's adrenaline rushed as he continued on a crash course with his adversaries. Mentally, he dared the Germans to stay where they were. He stared into the cockpit of the plane in his sights and flew headlong at the confused German pilots.

The Germans stayed their course, accepting the blatant dare. But the closer Bishop came, the more they began to worry. At the last minute they lost their nerve and swerved to their right. Bishop had anticipated the move and was ready.

Looping up and over in a barrel roll to his left, he gunned his engine until he was positioned under the enemy planes with his guns blazing. The cocky Canadian flew straight up and past them once more. He continued climbing above his opponents until his Nieuport fell backwards and went into a dive. Once more he came straight at the enemy at full throttle, with bullets flying. The game of chicken had gone to a second round.

Three times in all Bishop pulled the same manoeuvre. The Germans kept trying to get the better of him, but it was no use. The Canadian was out flying and outgunning all of them. Their planes, blowing smoke and leaking fuel, began limping, but Bishop kept coming, a manic single pilot against 6 enemy planes.

Von Richthofen had remained calm throughout the three attacks. He had been paying close attention to the way Bishop handled the aircraft and had figured out how to head him off. He sent his men in different directions at full speed. Bishop followed the two below him, exactly as the Baron had anticipated.

An Albatros D.III, such as Von Richthofen was flying when he and Bishop met. It had two machine guns to the Nieuport's one.

Unlike fighter pilots, observers in the kite balloons had parachutes.
Here, British observers prepare for test jumps. The chutes worked.

Bishop let loose his guns and sent one of the planes crashing and burning to the ground. The other, wounded, slowly circled, looking for a place to put down. Bishop's guns continued to slice into it, and this one also fell out of the sky. Bishop then dived at the remaining four fighters with guns blazing. There was no turning back. If he ran he could not escape. If he stayed he was grossly outnumbered, and his fuel was dangerously low.

The Red Baron had chosen his time for retaliation, and it was now. Closing in fast he calmly and coolly squeezed his trigger. To his amazement, he missed. Bishop had seen him coming and at the last second slid out of the way. Time and time again the Baron thought he had the tenacious Canadian, and each time Bishop bested the German ace. Bishop had one clear advantage — due to the Red Baron's fame Bishop knew a lot about his opponent. The Red Baron didn't know Bishop.

The game of chicken had graduated to cat and mouse. The planes buzzed above the ground, roaring and spinning, stalling and climbing. First Bishop chased after the Red Baron, then the Albatros flipped around and chased the Nieuport. The evasive tactics of both pilots worked in Bishop's favour. It bought him time. Finally his men showed up, and after taking care of the bombers they joined in the fray.

Low on fuel, the Baron reluctantly decided to leave the game and call it a draw. He signalled his men to head for home. In his mind, the battle had only just begun. He was certain he would win round two.

Bishop too, though he barely made it home on what was left in his fuel tank, was looking forward to another round. He didn't have long to wait.

A few days after that first thrilling encounter, Bishop took off from Filescamp Farm accompanied by Jack Scott. At almost the same time, the Red Baron and four of his fellow Albatros pilots took off from Douai. The two sides met near Drocourt, east of Lens, at approximately 2 p.m.

Scott and Bishop plunged into the middle of the five red planes. Two of the Albatroses cut across the Nieuports' flight paths and swung around behind them. The Baron opened fire with a sharp burst from his twin Spandau guns. The bullets peppered Scott's engine. Scott jerked his plane to the left and climbed out of the line of fire. Bishop swerved to his right as the Baron and one other German shot by above him. Then an

Albatros flashed in front of Bishop followed by another. Bishop was surrounded. Everywhere he looked scarlet planes were swooping and diving. It was a dangerous dance accompanied by the tattoo of bullets punching holes in canvas. The dance continued, the planes buzzing and the guns chattering. The Baron dipped under Bishop's belly and came around at him from the right. Bishop pushed his stick forward hard and banked over on his side as a stream of bullets smashed into the fuselage behind his seat. Seconds passed like minutes and Bishop thought for a second he'd been hit when he felt a bullet pass so close it ripped through the leather of his jacket.

The bullet sent Bishop into a blind fury. But he was still in the game and the adrenaline kicked in. He rolled his plane in a spiral to the right just as the Baron passed on the left. The undercarriages of the two biplanes barely slid past each other. Bishop didn't even hesitate. He banked sharply then dived, narrowly missing a stream of bullets from the Red Baron. Despite his aerobatics he still had one German on his tail, another diving from above and a third below him. The pattern was familiar to Bishop. The Baron had tried this one before and had almost got him. However, Bishop was setting the Germans up for a manoeuvre of his own.

The Baron looped around and flew at Bishop, weaving his plane from side to side. Bishop dived, then climbed, banked left and then right. He didn't intend to be an easy target as he swerved in all directions listening to the constant groaning of his biplane, which wasn't built for manoeuvres such as these. Storming at Bishop with a burst of speed, the Baron loosed off a stream of gunfire, and the bullets smashed into Bishop's instrument panel, drenching him in oil. He was

The Germans had Gotha G.IV bombers like this in service in April, 1917. Bishop was stalking two of them when the Red Baron arrived.

seething! His Nieuport was riddled with bullets and enough was enough. The Red Baron was about to taste the wrath of Billy Bishop.

Bishop pulled back on the control stick with a vengeance and gave the engine full throttle, and his plane headed straight up. Bishop rolled it over and kicked the rudder bar at the same time. The Baron's Albatros was now in his sights, and Bishop opened fire. The Baron had asked for a fight and Bishop was happy to oblige.

The Baron rolled his machine and dived straight for the ground with thick black smoke billowing from behind. Three Nieuports joined Bishop's fight and bullets flew at the German planes. The Baron's teammates realized they were outgunned and made for home, leaving the Baron to make his own way.

Bishop started to follow his adversary on his descent, but backed off after seeing the smoke spewing from the fuselage. For a brief moment Bishop thought he'd actually finished off the Red Baron. He waited for the crash. At the last moment the Baron levelled out, the smoke stopped and Von Richthofen flew off towards his home airbase. Again, it was a draw.

The aces never met again. Although it is widely believed that Bishop killed the Red Baron, it was not so. Manfred Von Richthofen died on April 21, 1918 in the skies over Vaux sur Somme, France. He was 25 years old. During a dogfight with a number of British planes a bullet pierced his heart. There were no other bullet marks on him or his plane. Another Canadian, Arthur "Roy" Brown, a notoriously bad shot, was credited with killing the infamous Red Baron.

Billy Bishop survived the First World War and became a legend in his own time. He remained in the air force after the war. Years later he travelled to Germany and paid his respects at the grave of Von Richthofen. While there, Bishop was made a member of the German Ace Association. He was, and is, the first and only foreign member of this elite association.

The daredevil who had tempted fate so many times in his youth eventually passed away peacefully in his sleep on September 11, 1956. He is buried in Greenwood Cemetery in Owen Sound, Ontario.

Chapter 6

THE CRUCIFIED CANADIAN: THE STORY OF SERGEANT HARRY BAND

The platoon leader of the 48th Highlanders, part of the Central Ontario Regiment of the Canadian Infantry, looked around the camp, counting heads. He couldn't locate Sergeant Harry Band, who had departed that morning with a squad of other men to scout the area for German activity.

The other men had returned, but no one had seen Harry, and his platoon leader was concerned. He didn't know if Harry had run into the enemy and been captured or killed, or whether he had simply deserted — after the last few days of bitter battles a number of men had gone absent without leave.

Harry never did return to camp and his absence remains a mystery to this day. But there is a horrific story that surrounds his death, a story that may be true or simply propaganda — it is hard to tell. It remains one of the most controversial mysteries of the Great War.

*The 48th Highlanders as they marched to the train in Toronto,
headed for overseas, in the rain. Harry Band is in there somewhere.*

The story starts at the second Battle of Ypres on April 22,
1915 in a meadow off the Poperinghe-Ypres road. After a brutal
battle for Hill 60, those men of the Queen Victoria Rifles who
remained alive were taking in the first signs of spring. They
were enjoying a respite from the fighting. Their casualties had
been high, but they had taken the hill and an exhausted elation
filled the air. Here and there men lay on the cool green grass
and watched the fluffy white clouds chase each other across
the blue sky. Some were peeling wet mouldy socks off swollen
and blistered feet. Stretching their fungus-laden toes in the
warmth of the sun felt like a luxury, and for a brief moment
they could almost forget the war, if not for the distant boom of
guns and the trembling of the earth beneath them.

The company cooks were preparing a meal and the smell drifted tantalisingly on the breeze. The men were far enough back from the front that digging in wasn't necessary, so huts were being erected. It was a rare treat and one the men were looking forward to — they would sleep that night off the ground, out of the mud and

Sgt. Harry Band, 15th Battalion, Canadian Infantry.

protected from the weather, the bugs and the vermin. Many were planning to give themselves a good scrubbing and to delouse their uniforms before bedding down.

They were to be disappointed. As the sun began to sink below the blackening horizon, this peaceful atmosphere was shattered by an increase of shellfire to the northwest. It seemed close, and each shell seemed louder than the one before. The men rose from their repose and struggled into their boots and helmets while they watched the fireworks in the sky and the manmade lightning that brightened the horizon. Suddenly, a mile away to the northeast, a massive shell burst in the heart of the stricken city of Ypres. The ground shuddered beneath their feet and dust blocked out the emerging stars. But it wasn't the bombardment that held their attention. With a sick dread building in the pit of their stomachs they watched an ominous yellow-grey smoke rolling across the landscape. Smoke was often used to hide troop activity, but not this kind of smoke. At first it settled in the French trenches, and men poured out of the earth like ants. Others tried to take their place but they too eventually turned and ran. The smoke continued rapidly towards the retreating troops, pushed along by the bursting of shells. Ahead of the cloud the British, French and Canadian troops all ran for their lives. Suddenly the road from the Yser Canal was filled with galloping horses and men yelling and beating their mounts to go faster. The men wore a crazed look. Some had pink froth drooling down their chins, and their eyes were red and weeping. The road became a seething mass of panic amidst a swirling pall of dust as men fled a terror that no one could explain. Their lungs were burning, their throats swollen and they were coughing up blood.

Hill 60 was formed of dirt dug up for a railway cutting. This is a view from a bridge over the cutting. As usual, there is mud.

In a front line trench on Hill 60.

The men of the Queen Victoria Rifles stood and stared, not understanding the crisis unfolding before them. They soon became aware of a pungent, nauseating smell that tickled their throats and made their eyes smart. The hordes of men running down the road were moaning and throwing away ammunition, rifles and equipment — anything that slowed their retreat. Vomit ran down their chests and with rasping voices and failing breath they yelled painfully: "Run! Run for your lives!"

Chlorine gas — the newest evil used by the Germans.

Officers yelled orders and the Queen Victoria Rifles were sent down the road in double-time into the fighting a mile away. The men were ordered to dig in and they fabricated makeshift gasmasks from woollen socks soaked with urine. They dug

German prisoners wear gas masks as they stretcher in a wounded Canadian. One officer, though, has decided not to wear his mask.

desperately on either side of the narrow roadway while shells pounded and bullets flew around them. The ground was wet, slick with blood and pooled rainwater. A shell detonated like thunder close by on the north side of the road and deafened them as the air filled with the filthy fumes of cordite. The living threw themselves face down against the sides of the partially dug ditches, oblivious to the mud. The shell had found two motor-gun teams, who were trying to find shelter in one of the ditches along the side of the road. Dirt, mud, fragments of scorched uniforms and human flesh flew through the air from the force of the blast. Above the sound of the nonstop shelling rose the sound of moaning so terrible it would haunt the survivors until their dying day. Then another shell, another direct hit and those still in one piece were splashed with blood and body parts and torn with shrapnel.

On the move again, one squad came across a nest of Germans who put up a fierce fight. In a frenzy of bullets and yelling, the Germans were slaughtered by the enraged British soldiers. More Germans came screaming at them in waves, and the British

Hill 60 from the front line. The fabric screens hide movement.

fired round after round until their gun barrels glowed red and were too hot to hold. They showed no mercy and took no prisoners. It didn't matter in those moments that the German use of chlorine gas was in retaliation for the Allies' use of mustard gas. Their rage recognized no arguments for fairness or tolerance. Their actions were governed by a baser instinct — an eye for an eye.

The next day the battle abated. Snipers still lay in wait for the unwary, but exhaustion swept over the troops on both sides, and many had no strength, emotionally or physically, to carry on the battle. Then the reports came down the line: German prisoners had been shot by the enraged Allied troops holding them. No one wanted to believe the reports, or admit the feelings that had gripped them during the last 24 hours. They hadn't killed unarmed men, but during the thick of the battle their comrades had killed rather than give the other side a chance to surrender. Given the opportunity, would they have killed prisoners as well? Could they have? Not one dared answer that question, even in his own mind.

True or not, the stories of prisoner slaughter spread throughout the British and Canadian lines. They also fell on German ears, and so the fate of Sergeant Harry Band was sealed.

Harry Band was born on August 12, 1885 in Montrose, Scotland. His family immigrated to Canada when Harry and his younger sister Elizabeth were teenagers. They made their home in Kelowna, British Columbia. Harry's older brother, James, remained in Scotland.

When the Great War broke out, Harry was working as a lineman with the Canadian Northern Railway, and volunteered as a firefighter. He was saving money, as he had plans to marry his childhood sweetheart, who was still living in Scotland, and bring her to Canada. He'd had military experience, having volunteered with the 48th Highlanders. The war was his chance to really fight and this 5' 11" man with sparkling brown eyes signed up quickly, enlisting with the Central Ontario Regiment, Canadian Infantry on September 18, 1914. In a few months he went overseas with the 15th Canadian Battalion, "C" company of the 48th Highlanders of Canada.

He underwent training in England, and during his leave he had a chance to visit Scotland and visit his girl, Isabella Ritchie, and his brother James Band, who still lived in Dundee. He planned on marrying Isabella as soon as the war would let him. She could then travel to Canada as a war bride, and he would follow after the war.

When the news came that he was shipping out, he made arrangements for his pay to be forwarded to Isabella. Almost a

The Second Battle of Ypres, 22 April to 25 May 1915, *3.71 by 5.98 metres, by war artist Richard Jack, 1916, unflinchingly shows the fight.*

year after signing up, Harry found himself stationed in France. By April 1915, he was fighting in Belgium.

On the front line, war was more than Harry had bargained for. The battle of Ypres was a nightmare. In a letter home he described pulling the corpse of one of his buddies out of the way so he could carry on the battle. He spoke of sleepless nights and horrific fighting. He told them he thought it was as bad as it could get.

He was mistaken.

On April 24, 1915, two days after the chlorine gas attack near the almost demolished town of Ypres, Sergeant Harry Band was sent on a scouting mission with seven other men. They split up in a small grove of trees around a deserted farmhouse. They were trying to locate pockets of resistance and were to report their findings back to their platoon.

The landscape seemed quiet and peaceful, almost as if the war had never happened. The small farm was quaint, ringed with a low-lying stone wall. Behind the old-fashioned house there was a barn and a ravaged kitchen garden. In the middle of the yard stood a scarecrow wearing an old hat, its soft, weathered fabric moving gently in the faint breeze. A crow cawed raucously from a nearby tree.

Perhaps Harry was lulled into a false sense of security by the serenity of the scene. Perhaps he had decided to lean comfortably against the warm stone wall close to the barn. Perhaps that's where the German soldiers saw him and surrounded him while he mused on home and other pleasant things. Harry was thrown to the ground, beaten with rifle butts and stomped by mud-caked boots. Rage, ignited by the stories of the merciless killing of German prisoners, fell on Harry Band that morning. He was their sacrifice, their message to the enemy. And he received no quarter, no mercy, no second thought.

Harry's limp, semi-conscious, bruised and bleeding body was dragged to the quaint barn door. Bayonets were unleashed, and as Harry was held against the wood his attackers looked into his eyes and spat curses as they systematically nailed him to the quaint barn door — through his eyes, his shoulders, his neck, his hands, his feet and his testicles. Harry became the German soldiers' message to the Allied forces.

George Barrie had taken refuge from the gas attack in the nearby village of St. Julien, in a farmhouse close to the woods. The Germans came through the village but George escaped from the house under fire and hid in a nearby drainage ditch. A group of German soldiers searched the house and barn near the ditch, and George stayed hidden until dark. When the enemy

Canadian Motor Machine Gun Brigade pauses alongside the Arras-Cambrai Road during the advance East of Arras, September 1918.

left, he decided to see what they had been up to at the barn. He saw a man in British uniform, apparently leaning against the barn door where the Germans had been standing. He was horrified when he realized that this young sergeant with maple leaves on his lapels was not leaning but was suspended off the ground, crucified to the door with eight bayonets. At the sergeant's feet lay his rifle, the only means of identifying him.

Barrie reported what he had seen to his platoon leader. After dark, a search party was sent to the area but no one could find the body. And without a body, no one could say for sure that Harry Band was dead. Harry never returned to his unit, however, and he was never seen again.

Miss Ursula Violet Chaloner, a British nurse and daughter of the first Baron Gisborough, wrote a note in July 1915, relaying comments made by one of her patients, Lance Corporal C.M. Brown. Brown, recovering from shrapnel wounds, had told Miss Chaloner about a Sergeant Harry Band, who "was crucified after a battle of Ypres on one of the doors of a barn with five bayonets in him." This note, along with a letter of condolence to Harry's sister Elizabeth, is the only evidence supporting George Barrie's account. Nevertheless, the gruesome story spread among the troops like wildfire and became one of the longest-enduring legends of World War I.

It eventually found its way into newspapers across Canada and the United States. The Germans categorically denied that the event had ever happened, and no one ever produced evidence beyond the statement of one eyewitness who hadn't been able to identify the victim or produce a body.

Harry Band was 29 years old when he was listed as "missing in action, presumed dead" on April 24, 1915. His name is inscribed on the Ypres (Menin Gate) Memorial.

Chapter 7
THE HERO OF THE
HALIFAX EXPLOSION

For 45-year-old Vincent Coleman, December 6, 1917 started out as simply another day's work at the Richmond train station in Halifax, Nova Scotia. Vince was one of two dispatchers working for the Canadian Government Railways that morning, and his day began early, at 6:30 a.m. The dispatchers controlled train activity on the main line into Halifax, which ran along the western shore of the Bedford Basin from Rockingham Station to the city's passenger terminal at the North Street Station at the corner of Barrington and North Streets.

Halifax has one of the world's largest natural ice-free harbours. In 1917, the harbour experienced a constant ebb and flow of wartime shipping. Convoys of ships belonging to Allied countries entered the port where they were loaded with munitions, troops and supplies bound for Europe. They assembled in the Bedford Basin and waited for orders to commence their

Troopships for the Atlantic were crowded. Here, SS Caledonia *leaves Saint John, NB.*

voyage. Destroyers, cruisers and ships of all sizes poured in and out of the harbour every day.

Ships belonging to neutral countries were required to moor offshore. Goods were loaded and unloaded where the ships were moored, and none of the men onboard were granted shore leave for fear of spying. The harbour was busy with boats transporting supplies and cargo out to the waiting vessels.

At 8:45 a.m. the *Mont-Blanc*, a French steamship filled with munitions, was entering the harbour. As a result of misunderstood signals *Mont-Blanc* collided with the unloaded Norwegian ship *Imo*, chartered by the Commission for Relief in Belgium in a part of the harbour known as the Narrows. Knowing that their ship was filled with explosives, including picric acid and dynamite, the crew abandoned her, expecting an explosion at any moment. *Mont-Blanc* was left to drift and, as she closed in on Pier 6 ten minutes after the collision, she burst into flames, sending black clouds of smoke billowing into the sky. People gathered along the shore to watch, not realizing the danger. Sailors who had abandoned the ship yelled the warning, and almost immediately dockyard fire alarm box number 83 at the corner of Room

Street and Campbell Road sounded.

Seeing the serious nature of the fire from his home, Mr. Constant Upham ran the short distance to his store, one of the few buildings with a telephone, and reported the fire to the surrounding fire stations.

Fire Chief Edward P. Condon and Deputy Chief William P. Brunt were next on the scene, arriving from Brunswick Street in the fire department's McLaughlin Roadster. By this time the fire had spread to the docks and the heat

The remnants of blast itself, probably taken mere seconds after the explosion.

was overwhelming. When he saw the magnitude of the fire, Chief Condon pulled the box 83 alarm again. Retired hose man John Spruin Sr. answered the second call from the station on Brunswick Street in a horse-drawn pumper, and hose man John H.E. Duggan attended with another horse-drawn firefighting wagon from the Isleville Street Station. At this point, none of the firemen knew there were munitions aboard *Mont-Blanc.* Nor did they know that the crew had abandoned the ship soon after the collision. They set to work

The Norwegian steamship Imo *(ex.* Runic *(I), 1889) beached on the Dartmouth shore after the explosion.*

to save the crew, who they believed were still onboard, and to prevent the fire from spreading any further.

Vince Coleman was working in the office when he saw a few sailors running by the window. He and a fellow worker stepped outside to see what all the commotion was about. They were told, "run for your life, the *Mont-Blanc* munitions ship is on fire. She'll blow the harbour to pieces."

The two men turned and started to run to safety. However, before Vince got very far he remembered that the 9:00 a.m. passenger train from Saint John, New Brunswick was due to arrive at the railyard within minutes. He turned around and ran back into the dispatch office. In a panic, he

The Mont-Blanc*'s anchor shaft, over 500 kg, flung nearly 4 km by the explosion, now preserved as a memorial in a Halifax park.*

hammered out an urgent telegraph message:

"Stop trains. Munitions ship on fire. Approaching Pier 6. Goodbye."

On receiving the message, the train, with 300 passengers onboard, stopped and waited at Rockingham. The message was also received all along the railway line and officials responded immediately by putting together crews to race to the aid of Halifax Harbour.

The *Mont-Blanc* munitions ship exploded at 9:04:35 a.m., about 25 minutes after the collision with *Imo*. Vince Coleman never made it to safety and was killed at his post as the blast ripped the harbour apart. Everyone at the scene of the fire died

Aftermath of the Halifax Explosion. The building on the left is Hillis & Sons Foundry.

immediately. John Spruin and John Duggan were both struck and killed by shrapnel enroute to the fire. Their horses were also killed.

A man named Billy Wells, a driver of one of the fire engines, was standing some distance from the vehicle at the time of the explosion. The powerful force of the blast blew his clothes off his body and stripped almost all the flesh off one arm.

Every building and structure in an area covering nearly 250 acres along the Halifax shore was destroyed. The north end of Halifax and the neighbouring community of Richmond were obliterated. Across the harbour from Halifax, on the Dartmouth shore, the small Mi'kmaq settlement in Tuft's Cove was also completely destroyed. The blast snapped trees, bent iron rails, demolished buildings, grounded vessels and threw fragments of the *Mont-Blanc* for miles. It also caused a tsunami in the harbour, and people were drowned and thrown around by the wave. Bodies hung from the windows of the devastated buildings. Some hung in the few trees that were still standing and others were washed into the harbour.

Soldiers engaged in rescue work after the Halifax Explosion.

The force of the blast shook buildings and overturned lighted stoves and lamps. Fires broke out all through the city, leaving entire streets burning. The casualty list grew longer. Volunteers from surrounding communities worked tirelessly and by evening most of the fires were contained. More than 325 acres of Halifax had been destroyed. The harbour itself was demolished. Houses and buildings as far as 10 miles away were damaged and windows broken. In Prince Edward Island, 130 miles away, people felt tremors from the blast.

Canada was at war. Concern that the blast had been caused by the Germans fuelled fear of another impending attack, and some citizens chose to evacuate the area. Others ignored the danger and worked feverishly to gain control of the situation. But their efforts were thwarted the following day

Factories, shops, warehouses, and dwellings all were smashed by the blast. This was probably a nice house, to judge by the bathtub.

when the temperature plunged and a blizzard brought 16 inches of snow. People still trapped in the rubble suffered through the bitter cold and some succumbed to it. The only positive effect of the blizzard was to put out any remaining fires.

There is no actual count of the deaths caused by the Halifax explosion. The toll is estimated at 2,000, but only 1,950 names appear in official records. An additional 6,000 were injured. More Nova Scotians were killed in the Halifax explosion than were killed on the battlefields of Europe.

Even though the figures are staggering, the tragedy would have been a great deal worse if it hadn't been for the sacrifice of Vince Coleman. He is honoured as a hero in Canadian history.

P. Vincent Coleman was survived by his wife Francis and is buried in Mount Olivet Cemetery in Halifax.

Chapter 8
IN FLANDERS FIELDS

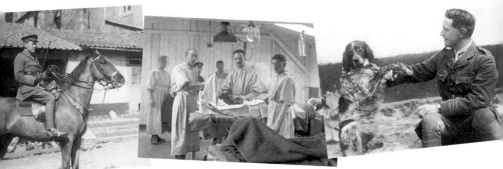

The scarlet poppy has been a symbol of remembrance for the fallen for as long as most people in Canada can remember. The poppy, however, was simply another common wildflower until a war-weary Canadian doctor penned a poem on a Flanders battlefield during World War I.

John McCrae was born in Guelph, Ontario on November 30, 1872. He studied medicine and served as a physician in the Boer war of 1899–1902. After the war, he returned to Canada and hoped he would never again have to witness men killing and maiming one another. But with the outbreak of war in 1914 his hopes were shattered. He felt it his duty to serve his country once more, even though he was in his early forties. Though he found war repugnant, he knew this fight for freedom was necessary. Wounded and dying men would need his abilities. He went overseas not

Lt.-Col. John McCrae on his horse, Bonfire.

only for his country, but also for the sake of the wounded.

John McCrae was single and childless, but he was close to his parents, siblings, nieces and nephews. It was hard to leave them, knowing that he might never return. He made a special effort to stay in touch with the children in his family by writing them letters as though they were from his horse. His trusty steed, *Bonfire*, who shipped out with him, even "signed" the letters with a hoof print.

Once overseas, John was appointed Brigade Surgeon with the rank of Major, second-in-command to the 1st Brigade of the Canadian Forces Artillery in France. By the beginning of April 1915 he was at his first assignment in Belgium, posted to the Ypres front line in an area traditionally called Flanders.

A Canadian doctor checks wounded Canadians before they leave an aid post near Lens, September 1917.

He was in charge of emergency medical care, pulling duty both in the medical tents and in the trenches.

Ypres was a German stronghold and the most heavily defended area along the western front. It saw the fiercest fighting and horrific loss of life.

It had rained incessantly that spring and the battlefield — on fields that had once grown grain — was a sea of shell-churned mud.

John knew he would never get used to the toll on human life and was devastated by what he saw. Men with wives and families were blown to pieces. Men who in peacetime lived by working the land lost arms and legs. Well-educated men, the scholars of their generation, suffered massive head traumas and became simple minded. Then there was the emotional carnage. Even strong, resilient men suffered from nightmares, the shakes and nervous twitches. Dr. John McCrae wondered if those who survived this hell would ever be able to adapt to normal life again.

The medics who brought the wounded to the doctors would tell John it was a miracle that any of them lived long enough to get to the medical unit. Men fell where they stood and lay bleeding in the mud with rats running over their prostrate forms. The medics did their best to get everyone out, dodging bullets and shells. Naturally, they evacuated the worst of the wounded first. The corpses had to wait. It wasn't unheard of for a corpse to lie in the mud at the feet of fighting soldiers for the duration of a battle, whether it was a few hours or a few days. By the time the medics reached these cadavers, they had to beat the rats off before loading them onto stretchers.

While doctors worked tirelessly to patch up the wounded, the men in the trenches continued to fight hour after hour. Whenever they had time, they dragged the wounded to one side so they could at least be made a little more comfortable. The wounded who could still walk would crawl out of the trenches and limp the 50 or so yards to the medical tent, where they waited in line for their turn. They usually waited for hours.

Inside the tent, saving life was the priority. Everything else — limbs, fingers or eyes — was less important. The physicians hated to make choices. At first, they would try to weigh what was best for the patient, but the sheer volume of casualties made hesitation a luxury they could not afford. Save this life, chop off this limb, and move on to the next victim.

Wounded Canadians at a Chaplain Service free coffee stall during the advance east of Arras, September 1918.

John hated it.

He didn't have time to stop and think about a soldier who had died, or even take a moment to mourn his passing. Mourning was another luxury he had taken for granted before the war. All he could do was push the grief to the back of his mind and focus on the task at hand. The time for grief would come later, and while hundreds would remain nameless to John, he would never forget them or stop grieving over their loss. In the meantime, he continued to sew ripped flesh, amputate useless limbs and pray for his patients' pain to be over.

Pain relief was a challenge at best. If the medical supply trucks got through, the wounded got chloroform. If the trucks

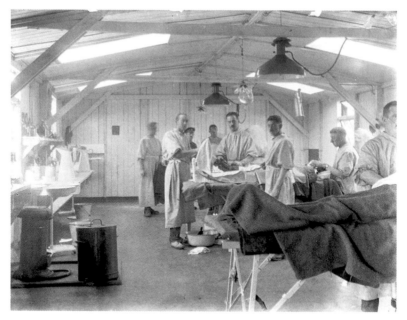

*The operating room, No. 3 Casualty Clearing Station, July 1916. If
wounded men got this far, they had a chance — but only a chance.*

were attacked or stuck in the mud the men had to make do
with liquor. If there was no liquor to drink the wounded would
be held down while the medical procedure was completed.
They screamed until they passed out from the pain.

John could still hear those screams when he closed
his eyes at night. He could hear them long after a patient
had died.

Even after a successful operation, there was no guarantee
of a safe recovery. Infections were of epidemic proportions and
the smell of gangrene tainted the air, mixed with the smell of
blood and explosives. At times, the doctors were thankful that
the medical aid station was a tent. The wind helped take away
the stench, but it was still overpowering.

John worked tirelessly. As the battles raged, the pile of limbs outside the makeshift surgery grew. When time and the enemy permitted, these limbs and soiled medical supplies were burned. Then the air smelled like a crematorium. The black ash of the dead drifted on the wind and landed on the living or mixed with the mud and water at the bottom of the trenches.

Thankfully, there were brief lulls in the fighting. During these periods John looked after other medical problems: rat bites, body lice, shell shock and the ever-present trench fever. The fever was spread by fleas that leaped from their host rats and onto the men. The sickness came with vomiting, diarrhoea, chills and delirium.

After a while, John had to close his mind to the horror of the dying and the hellish conditions of the living. He became numb. He felt he had seen the worst man could do to man. He believed the carnage had no more surprises for him.

Then, on April 22, during the second of three Battles of Ypres, the Germans did the unthinkable. They trucked in barrels of chlorine gas and turned it loose on their enemy.

The throats of the victims of gas attacks swelled so much that they could choke to death. They suffered terrible chemical burns and developed seeping sores in their mouths, noses and eyes. Some of the victims lost their sight. A whole new horror unfolded in the medical stations.

The medical staff did their best to ease the pain and treat the symptoms, but they had not been prepared for a weapon of this sort. Clean water for flushing eyes and cooling burns was in short supply. The men made gas masks from old socks soaked in urine and continued the fighting.

The Germans thought the gas attack would end the

battle, but they were wrong. It made the British and Allied soldiers angrier than ever, giving them strength they didn't know they possessed. Their tenacity, drained after the first shock of the gas, rebounded. With bleeding eyes and hacking coughs they manned their guns and continued to fight. When a man fell someone would take up the gun and fill the gap he left. They were no longer fighting only for their country or for an ideal. The fight had become bitterly personal.

For 16 days nonstop the Allies fought desperately to hold the line while the Germans threw everything they had at the troops. Focused only on the conflict, they refused to consider the possibility of the enemy breaking through. Every second of every day reverberated with the din of battle: whistling shells, deafening explosions, the chatter of machine gun fire, and — even worse — the cries and moans of the wounded. The air was thick with smoke from spent explosives. Exploding shells sent showers of dirt everywhere, and the smell of blood filled everyone's nostrils.

But they fought on.

No one slept during that battle. The soldiers just grabbed quick naps while standing at the guns and propped against the dirt walls of the trenches. They fought on continuously with the same filthy, mud-caked clothes glued to their skin and the same wet boots and socks on their feet. Rats feasted on corpses and then soiled the food supplies, so before long dysentery was added to their woes. With the fighting so fierce, the latrine was a luxury they could not afford. With gripping bowel pain, they remained at their stations throughout the battle and let nature take its course where they stood. They had no other choice.

Lt.-Col. John McCrae and his dog, Bonneau.

Hour after hour and day after day the Allied troops continued to meet the enemy force by force and blow for blow.

Doctor John McCrae didn't sleep for those 16 days. Like everyone else he had no time for anything but the battle — in his case, the battle to save lives. He ate his cold, meagre meals in seconds and washed the food down with dirty water.

Nearing the end of those horrible days, John McCrae discovered the body of a man he had grown up with in Guelph, Ontario. He thought he had become numb to the death around him, but he was wrong. This death almost broke him.

There was no time for proper mourning, no time for anything more than digging a shallow grave for his friend and marking it with a rough wooden cross.

An avenue of tents — No. 3 Casualty Clearing Station in July 1916, at Remy siding, France.

As John knelt beside the grave briefly in the cold, wet dirt, he thought his grief would overcome him completely. Then, out of the corner of his eye, beside this crude burial place, he saw a poppy, blood red and brilliant against the dark earth. There in the midst of horror grew beauty — life replacing death — a sight he knew he would never forget.

The day after he buried his friend, John noticed that the fields had blossomed. He looked out at the fields of poppies just beyond his medical station. The colour was so vibrant it almost hurt the eyes. While his eyes marvelled at such beauty, he wondered how anything could bloom in such a terrible place.

But bloom they did.

The poppies gave John an escape from the pain around him. The resilient flower became his symbol for all those who had died. He was so moved that he took time from his duties to write this poem, "In Flanders Fields".

In Flanders Fields the poppies blow
Between the crosses, row on row,
That mark our place; and in the sky
The larks, still bravely singing, fly
Scarce heard amid the guns below.
We are the Dead. Short days ago
We lived, felt dawn, saw sunset glow,
Loved, and were loved, and now we lie
In Flanders Fields.
Take up our quarrel with the foe:
To you from failing hands we throw
The torch, be yours to hold it high.
If ye break faith with us who die
We shall not sleep, though poppies grow
In Flanders Fields.

By May 25 both sides were completely exhausted and the second Battles of Ypres wound down to a climate of unease.

A few months later, John McCrae was transferred to No. 3 McGill Canadian General Hospital in Dannes-Cammiers, France, where he was appointed Chief of Medical Services shortly before the hospital opened in February 1916. Although this was a prestigious appointment, the hospital was just a group of very large tents covering 26 acres. During its existence, the facility would receive the wounded from the Somme, Vimy Ridge, the Third Battle of Ypres, Arras and Passchendaele.

These tents were adequate for the 1,500 plus patients during summer, but as soon as the weather turned cool and wet they were moved to some nearby ruins. However, moisture also pervaded the old buildings and John began to feel the effects of the prolonged exposure to the damp.

During the time John was stationed at Dannes-Cammiers, he wrote another poem, "The Anxious Dead". It was to be his last. He developed bronchitis, asthma, pneumonia and meningitis. John McCrae, physician, poet and patriot, died on January 18, 1918. He is buried in Wimereux Cemetery, north of Boulogne, not far from the fields of Flanders.

The day of John McCrae's funeral was bright and the ocean breeze blew gently. Bonfire, his horse, led the procession with John's riding boots placed backwards in the stirrups, a cavalry tradition to honour the fallen. The procession travelled soberly to the newly dug grave. There were no scarlet poppies growing around this mound of dirt. However, within a few short months the seeds of that resilient flower came to life and the plants began pushing their way up through the soil, as a proper tribute to the man whose memory would always be associated with them. Before long, they bloomed and blew "between the crosses row on row" in graveyards all over Europe, not only in Flanders Fields.

The poem "In Flanders Fields" became a success while John was still alive. It was first published by the English magazine *Punch* and grew in popularity throughout the Great War. It was even used on billboards advertising the sale of the first Victory Loan War Bonds in Canada during 1917.

The poppy has become the flower of remembrance for the war dead in many countries including Britain, France, the United States and Canada.

John McCrae's poem is read every year on Armistice Day, on the eleventh hour of the eleventh day of the eleventh month — lest we forget.

Chapter 9
A BEAR NAMED WINNIPEG

This story is about a bear, a bear that touched the lives of many and continues to touch the hearts and minds of children today. It is one of the most fascinating and endearing Canadian legends to come out of the World War I era.

In 1887, Harry Colebourn was born in Birmingham, England.

That same year, a few miles away, a five-year-old boy named Alan Alexander attended his first day at school. Alan enjoyed school and did very well over the years. In 1883, when he was 11, his teacher Herbert Wells helped him prepare for his scholarship exams. Alan won a Westminster mathematics scholarship and went on to university, where he studied English Literature.

Harry Colebourn immigrated to Canada at age 18 and settled in Toronto. In order to earn enough money for university, Harry worked at menial jobs such as selling fruit door-to-door and on the streets of Toronto, and worked as a deckhand on commercial vessels sailing the Great Lakes. Finally, in 1908, he had saved enough money to go to veterinary college in Guelph, Ontario and graduated on April 25, 1911 with a degree as a veterinary surgeon.

After a short trip home to England to visit his family, Dr. Harry Colebourn returned to Canada and went to work at the Department of Agriculture, Health of Animals Branch in Winnipeg, Manitoba as a veterinarian. Shortly after his move to Winnipeg, he joined the 18th Mounted Rifles as a volunteer militia officer and then went on to join the 34th Fort Garry Horse Regiment, where he became the veterinarian for the regiment's horses.

In 1914, a shot was fired that was felt around the world. It killed Archduke Franz Ferdinand of Austria, starting the conflict that quickly escalated into World War I. That same year, near White River, Ontario two other shots rang out from a hunter's gun, killing a mother black bear and one of her twin cubs.

These three shots shaped the future of both Harry Colebourn and Alan Alexander in a special and unique way.

When the war broke out in August 1914 Harry was already a trained officer and immediately enlisted in the regular army. He was given a leave of absence from the Department of Agriculture and boarded a train on August 23, 1914, bound for Valcartier, Quebec. While enroute, he was transferred from the 34th Fort Gary Horse to the Canadian Army Veterinary Corps.

On August 24, the train made a stop near White River, Ontario. Harry left the train in order to stretch his legs. Looking at his watch, he decided he had time to take a quick look at the small town. As he walked past a general store with a post office inside, he reached into his pocket to take out a letter he'd written on the train. Even though he hadn't been gone very long he decided to mail it. However, outside the general store something caught his eye. An old man was sitting on a bench, but what caught Harry's atten-

Capt. Harry Colebourn, Canadian Army Veterinary Corps.

tion was the very young black bear cub on a rope tied to the arm of the bench. Harry knelt down and the small bear nuzzled his wet nose into his hand, looking for food. The cub made a plaintive cry, and Harry's heart melted.

"This is a young one, where'd you get her?" Harry asked the man.

"I shot her mother and her brother," the hunter replied. "Somehow I couldn't bring myself to shoot her too. Don't know what I'll do with her though."

Harry looked into the cub's mouth and felt her coat along her ribs. She was young, too young to survive without her mother. He knew that if he walked away and got on the train without her she'd likely die. She licked his hand and looked up at him with her soft brown eyes. He sighed.

Harry Colebourn with Winnie the bear, in the Canadian training camp on Salisbury Plain, England.

"I'll give you $20 for her," Harry said. That was a great deal of money in 1914, and Harry was sure the man would take it without hesitation. He was right.

Forgetting his letter, Harry picked up the ball of black fur and ran for the train, which was now blowing its whistle impatiently. Harry named his bear *Winnipeg*, after his adopted home town in Manitoba.

On September 12, Harry was taken on strength by the Second Canadian Infantry Brigade Headquarters under the command of Lieutenant Colonel Arthur W. Currie. In Quebec, *Winnipeg* became a mascot for the regiment and the men nicknamed her "Winnie." Winnie grew strong and happy with all the loving attention the men bestowed on her. Some of her antics — like the time she raided the mess tent — brought a certain amount of disapproval from some of the officers. But even her worst mischief was eventually forgiven, and on October

3, 1914, when Harry was ordered to ship out, *Winnipeg* went with him.

At Salisbury camp, Winnie enjoys a treat.

They left from Gaspé Bay, Quebec on board the S.S. *Manitou* and arrived in Devonport, England. *Winnipeg* and Harry reported to the Second Canadian Infantry Brigade headquarters at Salisbury Plain, and *Winnipeg* became a mascot of the Canadian Army Veterinary Corps.

Winnipeg adapted well and was spoiled and indulged by the men. She followed them around faithfully. Many of them had their pictures taken with her, and she loved all the attention.

One day Harry was called into headquarters. He was told that they had orders to ship out, and as much as they all loved *Winnipeg*, an active war zone was no place for a loving bear. Harry was told to find a home for his bear.

Harry knew that this was coming. He had often wondered what he would do with the bear once the corps was ordered to battle. So Harry contacted London Zoo and asked them to take *Winnipeg* on loan. He said he couldn't part with her permanently, and that if he survived the war he would return to take her back home to Canada with him. The zoo authorities agreed, and Harry left her there on December 9, 1914 after a very emotional goodbye.

Whenever Harry took leave in England he always visited Winnie at her new home in the zoo. She was very happy there and especially loved the children, who rode on her back and

Harry Colebourn seems to be having a nice chat with Winnie, in the camp on Salisbury Plain.

played with her. Harry was always emotional when he had to leave her, even though he knew she was happy and well looked after. He missed her and looked forward to the end of the war.

Harry Colebourn survived the war, albeit with a scar on his scalp from a sniper bullet.

His first stop back in England was London Zoo. Winnie greeted him with hugs and groans and they played and wrestled. But for Harry this was not the reunion he had planned. Winnie had become a feature attraction for the many thousands of visitors and especially the young children, some of whom were permitted to feed her from a baby's bottle. He saw how the children loved her and how Winnie loved her life at the zoo. She was considered completely trustworthy by her keepers, who said that of all the bears they had in the zoo, Winnie was the only one they could trust with the children. Harry knew that it would be unfair to rip her from her home here and take her back to Canada, as much as he was going to miss her.

Harry said a heartbreaking final goodbye to *Winnipeg*, and in 1919 he donated her to London Zoo as a gesture of his appreciation for its efforts in caring for her during those four war years. He left for Canada with a heavy heart.

London Zoo held a dedication ceremony for Winnie and erected a plaque explaining that Winnie had been generously donated to the zoo by World War I veteran, Captain Harry Colebourn of the Canadian Army Veterinary Corps.

The statue of Harry Colebourn and Winnie the Bear at London Zoo.

The newspapers in England jumped on the story and numerous articles about Winnie appeared week after week. Visitors flocked to the zoo to see the antics of this remarkable bear and Winnie brought smiles to the faces of hundreds of children.

In the meantime, Alan Alexander had also grown up. He was now married and by 1924 he had a four-year-old son who loved to go to London Zoo. The little boy had two favourite animals at the zoo. One was a swan he named "Pooh," and the other was the gentle old bear Winnie, who did tricks for him every time he came. In fact, Alan's little boy was even allowed to go into Winnie's cage, where he fed her a bottle of condensed milk.

Christopher Robin was the name of Alan Alexander's little boy who was captivated by Winnie.

A. A. Milne in 1922.

Alan Alexander's last name was Milne. He was the A. A. Milne who wrote the stories and antics of a bear named *Winnie the Pooh*. And the orphan cub rescued by Harry Colebourn during that train stop in White River, Ontario was the original Winnie the Pooh. Alan's book quickly sold 7 million copies when it was published in 1926. Today, it is one of the world's best-known works of literature. (Incidentally, Alan Alexander's teacher, Herbert Wells, retired from teaching and became an author, writing classic science-fiction works such as *War of the Worlds* and *The Time Machine* — under the name H. G. Wells.)

Winnipeg, "Winnie" the bear, passed away on May 12, 1934 at the ripe old age of 20 years. Major Harry Colebourn passed away on September 24, 1947 in Winnipeg, Manitoba. He is buried in Brookside Cemetery, Plot 1312, in the Field of Honour.

A statue of a bear cub by sculptor Lorne McKean, with a plaque commemorating Winnie, stands at London Zoo. A statue of Harry and Winnie by sculptor William Epp stands in Winnipeg's Zoo.

Chapter 10
BROOKSY

According to newspaper articles, George Semperius Brooks, or "Brooksy" as he preferred to be called, towered above most men, standing 6 feet 2 1/2 inches tall. Brooksy was black. His skin was black, his eyes were black and the tightly curled hair on his head was black. It was the kind of hair that had earned the black men of the 10th Calvary in the United States the name "Buffalo Soldiers."

Brooksy knew about war — he claimed he had been a buffalo soldier during the Indian Wars. He also claimed he had served in the Spanish American War, the Cuban Campaign and the Civil War as an orderly to Ulysses S. Grant.

So why was this man, born a slave on a Kentucky farm, fighting as a Canadian in the hellhole that was France? Right now, in November of 1916, he was starving and foraging for food in a shelled-out, deserted village close to the Somme River.

Three black soldiers in a German dugout captured during the Canadian advance after Vimy, surrounded by German equipment.

He and the rest of his company from the 2nd Construction Battalion had gone without food for the last three days. The supply wagons couldn't get through, and all the men could do was fend for themselves. That was not an easy task, since the enemy had done what they could to strip the area of anything edible, warm, dry or comfortable.

Brooksy had come to Canada in 1911, settling on a farm in Westbourne, Manitoba. He had committed the cardinal sin, according to the United States' authorities. He had married a woman he deeply loved and who bore him a daughter. His wife was white. His child was of mixed race. It was illegal for the two races to marry and he had come home one day to find his wife butchered and his daughter close to death. She lingered

Two black Canadian soldiers take advantage of an opportunity to do their washing, September 1916.

a month before succumbing to her injuries. So Brooksy, filled with anger and grief, walked away from the country of his birth and embraced his adopted home of Canada.

Despite his terrible loss, Brooksy's warm eyes were framed with laugh lines, and there was usually a smile on his face. But those who knew him well saw the anger inside and it was this anger that had driven him to volunteer for the Canadian Army on May 6, 1916.

Like an estimated 1300 underage Canadian boys, George Brooks lied about his age in order to fight in France. But Brooksy was unique. Unlike those underage boys, he was 71 years old at the time of his enlistment, but swore that he was 40.

He wasn't the only black who fought in the Great War,

Portable field kitchen stoves went where the army went, setting up as close as possible to the front lines.

but very little has been written about these soldiers. The 2nd Construction was an all-black battalion whose officers were all white — except for one, Honorary Captain William A. White.

The 1,000 blacks were segregated in the army camps, on the ships and even on the battlefield. None of this was new for Brooksy. It had been the way of his world since the day he was born.

The injustice of segregation was never too far from his mind, although right now everything in Brooksy's being screamed out for food. Starvation was a bigger threat than the enemy at this point in time. What rubbed him most about the situation was that he was one of the company cooks.

Here he was — a cook — with no food to serve or eat. He found himself in a burned-out shack that at one time no doubt housed a family. Broken dishes crunched beneath his boots and his rifle was poised, ready for use. Unlike any other war he'd ever fought in before, now he was armed and he had already killed. He walked carefully, deliberately, with all senses alert. With one hand he opened those cupboards that still had doors, and rifled through garbage and rodent droppings for anything edible. His chest hurt, and with great effort he stifled the debilitating cough that threatened to overtake him.

Brooksy was suffering from pneumonia.

The service file of George S. Brooks, showing him to be 73 years old.

In a corner of the room, he sank his emaciated form to the floor. His once 193-pound body had filled his uniform when he had first put it on. Now the cloth hung loosely and he needed the belt, pulled through to the last notch, to keep his pants up. He leaned his back against a smoke-blackened wall and searched through a pile of clothes and broken pottery on the floor next to him.

Then he found it.

It was old, dry and hard. The heel of French bread was only the size of his fist, but he fell on it hungrily and tried to gnaw off a chunk. It defied him. He unscrewed his canteen and poured water on the crust, and once moistened, it was soft enough to eat. Brooksy was in Heaven. The bread was more delicious than the finest food in the best French restaurant. Nothing in his whole life had ever tasted as good.

He felt a tinge of guilt when the bread was gone and he had sucked his fingers to remove every trace. But he would keep searching, and he told himself he'd keep anything else he found for his comrades.

Then he doubled over with the cough, which could be denied no longer. His racking lungs were bursting, his throat was burning and a spasm gripped his chest, shooting stabs of hot pain throughout his body. He heaved and coughed, and black spots and stars swam before his eyes until thick green phlegm, mixed with blood, lay in a small puddle on the floor beside him.

Constant rain by day and frost at night, three months of damp feet and wet clothing, and the last three days spent without food had finally spelled the end of his tour.

Brooksy was taken to a hospital and sent back to England. While they treated him for pneumonia and bronchitis the doctors discovered his true age. He was eventually sent back to Canada and received a medical discharge in Winnipeg, Manitoba on September 14, 1918 at the age of 73.

On June 5, 1948, George S. Brooks passed away at Deer Lodge in Winnipeg, Manitoba. At the end of his tour, he had arguably been the oldest Canadian to have actively fought in World War I.

Appendix I

Historic Notes and Timeline

The Western Front

The Western Front was the name the Germans gave to a 420-mile series of defences stretching from the Swiss border to the North Sea in Belgium. Regardless of an intense offensive by the Allies, very little changed along this line of dugouts, trenches and barbed wire fences. The Western Front was strategically important as the Allies tried to push their way through in a "Race to the Sea."

The Ypres area of the Front in Belgium saw some of the deadliest fighting of the war, as did Flanders and the Somme River in France. Battles fought along the Western Front include the three battles of Ypres, the Battle of the Somme, and the Battle of Verdun. In all, 5.4 million men served on the Western Front and there were millions of casualties.

The Trenches

At the start of the war men fought in the open. When it became apparent that the war would not be "over by Christmas," and open-field fighting resulted in heavy casualties, both sides began to dig into the earth to provide cover where none existed. Eventually, short strips of open-topped tunnels appeared, and over time they became interlinked. These structures were called trenches, and the system of doing battle was referred to as "Trench Warfare."

The Allied trenches were about six feet deep and between three and six feet wide. Annexes big enough for five to eight men to sit in were dug adjacent to the trenches. These were called "rooms." Into the sides of the walls of these rooms the men dug sleeping holes, which were appropriately called "dugouts." Privately, the soldiers called them "graves" as the floor and ceiling were dirt, and they were closed in on three sides.

The dirt from digging the trenches was piled high on the enemy's side and made into a parapet where guns were mounted. To get to the guns, the men had to either scramble up the side of the wall of dirt or use a short ladder if they had time to build one.

If the line held for long enough, the men made improvements. The first thing they did was lay boards along the bottom of the trenches to keep their feet out of the water. They also put boards across the top of the rooms as makeshift roofs. Of course, one shell would destroy everything.

Some of the longest-lasting lines had trauma hospitals — simply a few tents — about 100 yards behind the trenches. Otherwise, the wounded were patched up quickly and transported to the nearest hospital, which could be as far as 30 miles away.

The German trenching system was more complex — deeper and wider, with underground rooms. They had the home-front advantage.

Perhaps the words of Otto Dix, the German Expressionist painter sum up trench warfare best: "Lice, rats, barbed wire, fleas, shells, bombs, underground caves, corpses, blood, liquor, mice, cats, artillery, filth, bullets, mortars, fire, steel: that is what war is . . . "

APPENDIX I

Casualties

Country	Military Deaths	Civilian Deaths	Military Wounded
Allied Powers			
Australia	61,928		152,171
Belgium	45,550	92,000	44,686
Canada	64,944		173,00
France	1,368,000	500,000	4,266,000
Greece	26,000	150,000	21,000
India	74,187		69,214
Italy	680,000	1,021,000	953,886
Japan	1,344		907
Montenegro	3,000		10,000
New Zealand	18,050		41,317
Portugal	8,145	220,000	13,751
Romania	300,000	430,000	120,000
Russia	1,700,000	1,500,000	4,950,000
Serbia	275,000	450,000	133,148
South Africa	9,463		12,029
United Kingdom	885,138	292,000	1,663,435
Totals	5,520,749	4,655,000	12,468,844
Central Powers			
Austria-Hungary	1,200,000	467,000	3,620,000
Bulgaria	87,500	100,000	152,390
Germany	1,935,000	624,000	4,247,143
Ottoman Empire	725,000	4,200,000	400,000
Totals	3,947,500	5,391,000	8,419,533
Neutral Nations			
Norway		1,892	
Totals		1,892	

The last Commonwealth soldier to be killed during World War I was a Canadian, George Lawrence Price. A German machine gunner shot him at the village of Havre, just two minutes before the Armistice was signed. Price was born in Nova Scotia, but lived in Moose Jaw, Saskatchewan before the war.

Sources of casualty statistics: *The Great War and the Shaping of the 20th Century* by Jay Winter and Blaine Baggett, published by Penguin Books, 1996, www.firstworldwar.com, Veteran's Affairs Canada and www.gwpda.org.

Appendix II

Battles Featured in These Stories

Name and Date of Battle	Title of Story
First Battle of Ypres Octber 14 – November 22, 1914	*Prologue,* *Rita Simpson's Story*
Battle of the Somme July 1 – Novmber 19, 1916	*The Danger Tree*
Second Battle of Passchendaele Ridge October 26 – November 6, 1917	*Comrade in White*
First Occurence of Chlorine Gas during the Second Battle of Ypres April 22, 1915 (First use of Chlorine gas by the Germans)	*The Crucified Canadian,* *In Flanders Fields*

ACKNOWLEDGEMENTS

The author would like to thank the following: Candace Boily for the story of her uncle, Edgar Simpson; Brian Jenkins for the story of Chrystie Jenkins; Cynthia Cramer for the story of the Comrade in White; the Department of Veterans Affairs and Collections Canada for access to Service records; the War Graves Commission for the grave information of various Canadian Veterans; Manitoba Archives for the information about Winnie the Bear and Harry Colebourn; and the Maritime Museum of the Atlantic for information about the Halifax Explosion. The quote "Stop trains. Munitions ship on fire. Approaching Pier 6. Goodbye" was drawn from The Great War and the Shaping of the 20th Century.

SELECT BIBLIOGRAPHY

Printed Material:

Arthur, Max. *Forgotten Voices of the Great War*. London: Ebury Press, Random House, 2002.

Bishop, William Arthur. *The Courage of the Early Morning*. Toronto: McClelland and Stewart, 1965.

Collections Canada. Service Records of Harry Band, Harry Banks, William (Billy) Bishop, George S. Brooks, Harry Colebourn, Delbert Cramer, Thomas Arthur Cramer, Chrystie Jenkins, John McCrae, and Edgar Simpson.

Collections Canada. *The Story of John McCrae*. www.collection-scanada.gc.ca

Glasner, Joyce. *The Halifax Explosion: Surviving the Blast that Shook a Nation*. Canmore: Altitude Press, 2003.

MacDonald, Laura M. *Curse of the Narrows: The Halifax Explosion 1917*. Scarborough: Harper Collins, 2005.

MacFarlane, David. *The Danger Tree*. New York: Walker & Company, 1991.

Mackenzie, Donald A. *From All the Fronts*. New York: Frederick A. Stokes Company, 1935.

Nova Scotia Archives & Records Management. *Halifax Explosion Remembrance Book*.

Palmer, Svetlana & Wallis, Sarah. *A War in Words*. London: Simon & Schuster (UK), 2003.

Purdam, C.B., ed. *Everyman at War*. London: J. M. Dent, 1930.

Reynolds, Quentin. *They Fought for the Sky*. London: Rinehart & Company, 1957.

Springs, Elliott White. *War Birds: Diary of an Unknown Aviator.* London: John Hamilton Ltd., 1925.

Stark, Rudolph. *Wings of War.* London: John Hamilton Ltd., 1933.

Websites:

www.angelfire.com

www.ww1battlefields.co.uk

Canada War Graves Commission @ www.cwgc.org

www.canadaka.net/quotes_list

www.collectionscanada.gc.ca

www.heritage.nf.ca

www.vac-acc.gc.ca

www.winniethepooh.co.uk